SETTLE-CARLISLE
STEAM
FROM LINESIDE TO FOOTPLATE

West Country Pacific No. 34092 *City of Wells* is highlighted passing Culgaith with a SLOA sponsored Cumbrian Mountain Pullman on the 13th February 1982. This occasion was the locomotive's inaugural southbound run on the line.

CONTENTS

Standards 75014 and 70000 *Britannia* at Ais Gill, 31st March 1995

FOREWORD — SETTLE TO CARLISLE
STEAM OVER THE DRAG

by R.H.N. Hardy

I was in my fifties when I first came across the Long Drag and I was never the same again. As a child, it was first the LB&SCR, then the LNWR, then the Great Central and it's engines. By the time I started on the LNER in Jan 1941, it was not to Gorton but at Doncaster which was the place to go and there were GC engines and, more important ex GC men, everywhere in the Southern Area which extended north to Copley Hill, Bradford, Brunswick and Walton-on-the-Hill. But the Midland? I had no time for it and never had even as a boy let alone a young railwayman. To an LNER Southern Area man in Bradford, Manningham might as well have been on the moon although we had a rough idea that Holbeck shed in Leeds had something to do with the Midland. As for the Settle-Carlisle, there had been trials soon after the 1923 Grouping and I did read somewhere that they had been rigged in favour of the Midland engines: anyhow the LMS was flooded with Fowler designs and I thought very little of them although the old M&GN men got amazing work out of their Johnson bogies and, come to that, the GN "W"s after 1936, work of which the main line men would have been proud.. But later on, I read Red for Danger, again and again until the Settle-Carlisle had entered my soul and each scene and incident is etched in my mind. But although as the newly appointed Divisional Manager Liverpool, I was on 5110 on that last steam job from Liverpool to Manchester and although the Chief Inspector, the late John Hughes wanted me to go through

A group which includes support crew members from the A4 Locomotive Society and BR staff pose in front of 4498 *Sir Nigel Gresley* at Appleby whilst waiting to work forward a Cumbrian Mountain Express in 1982. This occasion was the final steam turn for Chief Traction Inspector George Gordon before his retirement from British Railways.

L to R: Robert Riddick, Terry Wealleans, Julian Riddick, John Graham, Norman Hugill, George Gordon, Eddie Gibbons, Ian Howson (BR fireman), Davie Hine (BR driver), a P-way Ganger, Ben Hervey-Bathurst, and Dick Hardy. Photo: R.H.N. Hardy

to Carlisle on 70013 to help out, I was in the middle of moving house from the south and had to get home to Burton-in-Wirral to help the "Guv'nor".: only a couple of miles from the Great Central line from Bidston and that is typical of Merseyside where your staff might come from three of the four great railways and, of course, from the Mersey Railway.

So it was not until after 1976 that I set foot on the Drag and with engines to which I was well used, 4771, 4472 and 4498. Now there was a trio for you and it was on "*Green Arrow*" that I made my first journey in the Down direction and I was completely hooked: and as I look through this splendid book, I also see engines with which I have had very little to do, the Duchess for example and what tremendous power there was there, the ideal engine for a mechanical stoker, given the sort of coal that the French used in their stoker-fired engines. There are scenes from every vantage point by or near the lineside as well as by or on the engines with driver, fireman or inspector and frequently the support crews, of which the author was a member, on which so much depended. And there was the other-side of the coin if you look at page 53 and you will see the great "*Mallard*" brought low and at a standstill with smoke drifting from the chimney. I never had to look at

the caption, there she was with barely enough steam to work the blower and there she would stay filling the boiler and trying to raise steam for ten or fifteen minutes. I have had close on 70 years of firing engines and have stopped seventeen times, once going downhill by Tong Cemetary at 1 in 100, a right place for a blow-up and I stopped with Driver Joe Oglesby, a splendid "Grinder", three times on the climb from Sheffield to Dunford Bridge with a clapped-out K3 in 1944 and a boiler 26 days overdue for a washout.. It is an awful feeling when the power gradually fades away and the brake begins to rub and you come to a stand and until the blower catches hold of the fire, one feels one is there for ever. But even then don't go until you have full boiler pressure and a good fire and plenty of water in the boiler. So there they are with 4468 and it is a unique picture. There is so much to capture the imagination in this book of sensible and interesting text, full and informative captions (which can make or mar a book) and excellent photography.

In the summer of 1980, I made a journey over the Drag that will live with me for ever. It was before the days of Mike Notley's Blue Riband so it was not a particularly fast journey by comparison but I had the honour of firing to an ex-LNER man who had come from St Margarets to the

Driver Jim Lister (right) is pictured with his fireman Gordon Hodgson as they await NRM support crew members to complete a last minute repair to Coronation pacific 46229 *Duchess of Hamilton* at Carlisle Upperby on 26th October 1985. The group seen on the right includes: Chief Traction Inspector Ron Gerrard (second left), and John Duncan (extreme right), who was to become CME to SLOA in 1993.

old NBR shed at Carlisle Canal and what he didn't know about working an A3 over a heavy road was not worth knowing. This, of course, was Jimmy Lister and I had had plenty of time to prepare my fire at Appleby and seek his advice. The author's brother, Geoff, was the booked fireman whilst in charge of the support crew based on Carnforth was that old spell-binder with an engine, the retired Chief Inspector of the Eastern Region, Les Richards, an NER man who could be a bit sharp about LMS methods. George Gordon was the inspector and as far as Appleby, Kenny Stubbs was the nominal driver but George Gordon had told me to get on with the job and I was very much at home on this lovely old engine, built the same year as I was born. Somewhere along the line, George crossed the cab and tripped falling on and damaging his shoulder. After rubbing it a bit, he carried on and we thought no more about it. Jim and his mate had come aboard at Appleby and our journey up the hill was perfect. The exhaust injector was turned on immediately the steam pressure approached the red line after the first firing and I never shut it off until we were near the top of the hill to let the water down and avoid blowing-off at Garsdale. Jim was so consistent and correct in everything he did that my task was a joy and we must have impressed the visitors(one of whom was Terry Miller, my old Chief at Stratford) who came through the corridor tender, as a pretty fair team. I was then in my last job, before retirement, at BR HQ at Marylebone but Jim had no idea where I had sprung from or who I was hence his unforgettable remark after we had stopped "Well. Mr Hardy, I don't know who you are but you are a credit to your profession" but so were you, Jim and it was an honour to fire for you. And George Gordon? That remarkable man, who did so much for the success of the Settle-Carlisle services, did the driving to Hellifield and then got the best out of 5407, the incomparable Paddy Smith's splendid old "knock-john" almost up to B1 standard, between Hellifield and Carnforth. To get home to Carlisle, George had to continue to Lancaster where he had begun to feel the effects of his injury: he telephoned his daughter who I believe was a nurse and on arrival at the Citadel, was whisked straight off to hospital: he was off work for three months but he had seen the day's work through and that is what mattered to him- a real railwayman.

I knew some of the owners or those in charge of these preserved locomotives but I was to know them better by 1987 when I was asked to put myself forward as Chairman of SLOA which I did with some reluctance for I was deep into retirement and I had some misgivings. When I got used to the job, I realised that I should treat the owners as if they were actual railwaymen and what they undertook to do must be done as promised. David Ward who was responsible for the steam operation on BR has received his share of criticism in person and in the press and I am delighted that in this book, the author paints a true picture of David's worth. He and I used to have a good set-to once a year but we worked very closely to-

gether. I had both Michael Draper and Bernard Staite to hold my hand for it is one thing being a professional railwayman and another controlling the destinies of owners who have achieved great things and know it. It was great but I tell you this, once or twice we were on a knife's edge when certain senior BR officers were gunning for steam and it was my job, when they cut up rough and David was on the rack, to have the answers and be a step ahead and also a nice line in counter argument for one still knew exactly where to go on BR to get the information that would knob-stick the critics: I have still have some of the papers!

During my time as Chairman, for a short time, we had John Bellwood as Chief Engineer and then John Peck of York, a distinguished LNER locomotive engineer and a great friend. We retired from SLOA on the same unforgettable day in January 1993 and then came Brell Ewart as Chairman and, as Chief Engineer, John Duncan who lives in Carlisle and had worked there for BR towards the end of his career. He was Gorton trained, worked in running sheds in this country, then emigrated to Canada and had three and half years in the Running Sheds at Calgary before coming home again and what a wealth of creative and practical experience was available to SLOA and so frequently put to the test over the "Drag". On May 7th 1994, the Maunsell S15 "King Arthur Goods", 828 had worked from Carlisle over the Drag with Brian Hayton and that skilled "JCB operator" amongst firemen, Paul Kane and reached Farington Junction where it unhooked, ran round it's support coach and moved off tender-first to Blackburn en route to Keighley and the K&WV Railway. John Duncan had travelled in the coach on his way to Keighley when there was a tremendous jolt and the train stopped dead when entering the loop at Blackburn to take water. Expecting a derailment, John jumped down, went forward and found all in order but caught sight of the left side lifting link of the Walchaerts valve gear broken in two pieces. The LH side therefore dropped into fore-gear and the right side was held in back gear which stopped the job. However John and his crew set about making the engine moveable by centralising the reversing shaft and wedging wooden track keys in the quadrant to get 828 off the running line. They then measured pieces of wood to replace the keys and lashed the quadrant and it's packing with twine after which, with the help of a pinch bar or two, they set off for Keighley on one cylinder in full back gear. At Clitheroe they were stopped and told that the South Junction box at Hellifield was shut. It had to be opened and eventually the Hellifield S&T Inspector turned out and opened up at the South. Meanwhile a lady living near the line gave them tea and scones until they got the road and away they went to Hellifield where after a bit of manoeuvring, they set off along the main line next stop Keighley but a 20 mph speed order at Skipton, nipping along nice and steady at about 50mph and sounding like a Webb Compound with two beats to the bar. The Skipton crew got them across onto the Worth Valley and at 1.30 am, the support crew and railway staff settled down to a gammon steak supper and spent the rest of the night sleeping in the support coach. John had had a similar experience with a Black 5 so he knew the form and here was first class practical railway work at it's best from all concerned..

So the Long Drag is still there and will be in my lifetime and long after for sure and it is worth remembering the

Photo: Ken Armstrong

splendid part played by a senior BR Officer who had worked with me at Liverpool, a certain Ron Cotton who came to Liverpool in 1971 as our Passenger Manager and his responsibilities included the generation of passenger business by often unorthodox and extremely effective methods. The Merseyrail concept was very much his idea and when we put the name on the stock, there were those in high places who, with one or two understanding exceptions, did not approve at all. But the concept was successful whereupon the doubters jumped on the band-wagon with a flourish of trumpets. After I left Liverpool in 1973, Ron carried on until the Divisions were wound up when some genius appointed him to organise the closure of the Settle-Carlisle. But he did no such thing and he had reached a point in his career where he could make it his business to have a pretty free hand so let us be sure that Ron's work is always appreciated and that the Long Drag will be there for years to come to provide the steam locomotive and it's crews with that wonderful challenge amid the equally exciting and glorious Pennine countryside.

CALVERLEY–CARLISLE **GRADIENT PROFILE**

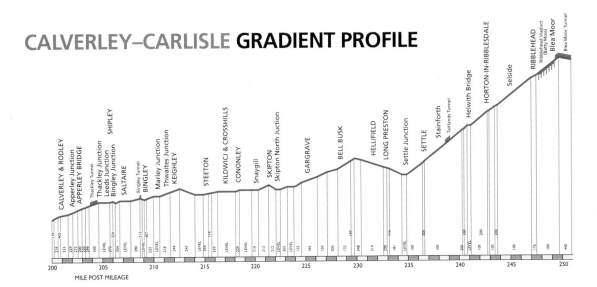

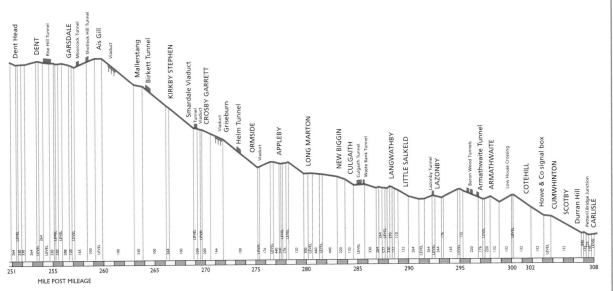

INTRODUCTION

Easter week-end, 1978, marked the return of the steam locomotive to the Settle-Carlisle Railway (S&C) after an absence of ten years, when former LNER class V2 No. 4771 *Green Arrow* departed Leeds with 'The Norfolkman' bound for Carlisle. For those who witnessed that momentous occasion, few could have envisaged that by the year 2008, we would have had thirty unprecedented years of steam-hauled charter trains on one of the most iconic lines in the country. Although the campaign to return steam to the national rail network had become reality during 1971, it was to be a further seven years before the signals at Settle Junction were pulled off to allow *Green Arrow*'s passage onto the S&C, an occasion that was to herald three decades of activity on a line that can justifiably be described as the finest theatre in the country for steam locomotive performance.

The Settle-Carlisle line was built by the Midland Railway (MR) and opened for passenger traffic in 1876. The mere fact that it was built at all was due to nothing more than a fall-out with bitter rival, the London & North Western Railway (LNWR) after they had refused the MR running rights over their lines which would have enabled the Derby based company to reach Carlisle thereby gaining access to what they considered to be lucrative Scottish traffic.

This refusal resulted in the MR seeking its own route to the Border City, a decision that led to the building of the S&C, a project that would take nearly seven years to complete, and undertaken by navvies armed with nothing more than pick and shovel. Such were the geological obstacles faced by their surveying engineer, Charles Stanley Sharland, the company was forced into the construction of no fewer than 325 bridges, 21 viaducts and 14 tunnels over the routes modest 72 mile length, and with a ruling gradient of 1 in 100, the Midland Railway had built a line that would test the capabilities of steam locomotives and their crews to the maximum as they battled against the elements to reach the summit at Ais Gill.

The contrast in landscape along the route is quite marked, as a lush Eden Valley gives way to what can be best described as a rugged and hostile environment where the line climbs high up into the Pennines to surmount the summit at 1,169 feet above sea level. The most dramatic section of the line is undoubtedly the 5 mile stretch between Ribblehead and Dent where the Midland pioneers were faced with building several major engineering marvels in order to conquest this inhospitable terrain: Ribblehead Viaduct; the most dominant feature on the line where 24 arches span 440 yards, Blea Moor tunnel; 2,629 yards long and 500 feet below

The peace and tranquillity of a desolate Blea Moor is briefly disturbed by the approach of a northbound goods hauled by Stanier 8F No. 48666 as it nears the end of the 15 mile climb from Settle Junction on the 21st September 1966. Standard class 9 No. 92161 waits patiently for a favourable signal prior to resuming its journey with an up anhydrite train. This image gives a good illustration of a mid 1960s scene on the S&C when goods traffic was still predominantly in the hands of steam, a situation that was to last until the end of 1967. Photo: Peter Fitton

ground, Dent Head Viaduct; 177 yards long and 100 feet high and the majestic Arten Gill Viaduct; 220 yards long and 117 feet high.

Both Ribblehead Viaduct and Blea Moor tunnel took five years to complete, and as one would have expected, it was the latter that proved the most costly – in lives, as well as finance. Huge numbers of navvies lost their lives in that area alone, some of whom were simply buried amongst the spoil heap near to the tunnel's northern portal. The makeshift gravestones situated there are a poignant reminder of the human sacrifice that was made to build the Settle to Carlisle Railway.

Although the intention of the Midland Railway was to link the Midlands with Scotland's industrial heartlands, the traffic on the S&C never really reached the high levels anticipated. The same can be said of the British Railways era, and with the scarcity of traffic using the line, it was little wonder that BR chose the route to host a number of controlled power output trials in the 1950s. Of course in those days steam power dominated the scene but this was to change in the early 1960s when the two principle express passenger trains, 'The Waverley' and 'The Thames-Clyde Express' became diesel-hauled. Goods traffic remained predominantly in the hands of steam and the S&C was eventually to become one of the last main line routes in

the country where the common steam locomotive could still be seen in everyday use. That relationship eventually came to an end with the closure of Carlisle Kingmoor steam shed on 31st December 1967.

Although steam traction was to linger for a further few months in other parts of the north-west, its final demise by British Railways took place on the 11th August 1968 with the running of a special train with the reporting number 1T57. Otherwise known as the 'Fifteen Guinea Special', this commemorative train ran between Liverpool and Carlisle and it was fitting that part of the route was to include the S&C, a line that had been associated with the steam locomotive for nearly one hundred years. As one would expect for such an occasion, crowds flocked to witness the events of that final day, but few, if any, could have foreseen that within ten years steam would return to regularly work over the line, known affectionately by many as 'The Long Drag'.

Although the new steam era was to belong to the preserved locomotive, their initial visits to the line actually began during the mid 1960s when examples such as *Flying Scotsman*, *Sir Nigel Gresley*, *Bittern* and *Clun Castle* hauled charter trains over the route into Carlisle. With the BR steam years coming to a close, a number of preservation societies had been formed

From a class of 191 locomotives, Jubilee 45562 *Alberta* eventually became the last one to be withdrawn from BR service. Allocated to Leeds Holbeck for many years, the locomotive was a regular performer on the S&C and along with the other two survivors: 45593 *Kolhapur* and 45697 *Achilles*, it was regularly diagrammed express passenger workings over the line right up to the end of her working life in November 1967. Out of the trio of Jubilees that kept enthusiasts enthralled with their eleventh-hour performances on the S&C, many hoped that *Alberta* would be saved, but as it turned out, 45593 *Kolhapur* was the one chosen to be preserved. Photo: Ken Armstrong

Privately owned preserved steam locomotives first began to appear on the S&C in the mid 1960s, and probably the most unusual one to visit the line before the end of BR steam was former GWR Castle No. 7029 *Clun Castle*. After having hauled a York to Carlisle charter train via the S&C on 30th September 1967, the locomotive is pictured at an untidy disposal road at Kingmoor shed. Closure of the depot was a mere twelve weeks away. Photo: Ken Armstrong

with the intention of securing a steam locomotive of their preferred choice. Some groups were fortunate in that they had the financial resource to purchase direct from BR, at least in that way they obtained a complete and probably steamable locomotive. Groups that had waited until after 1968, were forced into buying one of the 200 steam locomotives languishing in a South Wales scrap-yard, some of which could be best described as 'rusting hulks'. Going down that particular path usually involved a long and costly restoration project, but it was these pioneering private owners however, together with the management at the National Railway Museum, that led the way in returning steam to the main line once the infamous steam ban had been lifted by a very cautious BR.

Since the appearance of the first preserved steam locomotive to the S&C in 1978, steam activity has more or less become common-place as first BR, then subsequent train operators, acknowledged the revenue earning potential of the line which passes through one of the most scenic parts of the country. This attraction, coupled with the gruelling reputation that the line possesses, never ceases to entice owning groups of today's steam fleet to look upon the S&C as the ultimate test, and since 1978, it is my belief, that no fewer than forty-eight different steam locomotives have traversed the route, some with glory whilst others have not been so fortunate.

My involvement with the Settle-Carlisle line is reflected in the title of this book - from lineside to footplate. Hav-ing photographed steam workings during the 1960s in my home city of Carlisle and beyond, I was like many who followed that discipline, in that once steam had finished, that was it. Having no interest whatsoever in the modern railway scene, I drifted away from the subject completely, and although I became aware that preserved steam locomotives were running into Carlisle from 1978, I wasn't at all tempted to resume my acquaintance with them until the appearance of a certain class J36 engine by the name of *Maude*.

The first steam shed that I visited as a youngster was the Canal shed in Carlisle, and since that historic occasion, I have had this avid attraction to all things North British (NB). In addition to other NB locomotives, the Canal still had four class J36 engines on its books at the turn of 1960, and I would observe these diminutive 0-6-0 tender engines working lengthy transfer (trip) goods trains between the various yards in and around Carlisle. They were all withdrawn from service in the early 1960s, but I came across the class once again during 1965/66 visits to the Fife area where a small number were to be found still gainfully employed. To make my association with *Maude* even stronger, I had travelled on a J36 hauled railtour during 1966 around the Edinburgh area, the proceeds of which were to go to the purchase of the said *Maude*, and if all of that wasn't enough to make me go to see the celebrity J36 on its epic journey over the S&C in 1980, another, but real reason to see the locomotive that I had

The closure of Kingmoor steam shed on the 31st December 1967 brought to an end 92 years of daily steam activity on the Settle to Carlisle railway; Leeds Holbeck shed had succumbed to closure some three months earlier. This 1967 view of Kingmoor is dominated by Britannia No. 70013 *Oliver Cromwell* which was the last steam locomotive to be overhauled at Crewe Works in 1967 prior to its return to traffic at the Carlisle shed during February of that year. Upon closure of Kingmoor, 70013 was transferred to Carnforth for it to be kept available for special trains which included the last ever BR steam-hauled passenger train. Photo: Ken Armstrong

obviously saved from the cutter's torch was the fact that my brother had been rostered as fireman that day.

If ever a day was a turning point that was it. From that moment on, I was back behind the camera photographing steam on the S&C, but more than that, within five years I too would be travelling on the footplate of a steam locomotive across the former Midland line. The transition from one side of the fence to the other began innocuously enough with the purchase of a Christmas draw ticket!

During October 1982, class 5X No. 5690 *Leander* worked a double trip on the S&C. Although light was failing, I decided to go to Armathwaite to see it on the return journey and it was there that I was accosted by a couple of members of the locomotive's support crew who were selling raffle tickets to raise funds towards the upkeep of the engine. I bought a few of their tickets and thought no more about it until I visited the Upperby depot a few months later to see the locomotive being prepared for a run the following day. I met the same crew members who I had seen at Armathwaite and jokingly enquired if I had won the draw. It was obvious that I hadn't, but that didn't prevent them from inviting me to join them cleaning the engine. Many would have politely declined, but I accepted the offer, and returned home to obtain more suitable clothing for the challenge that lay ahead. As a result of that day's action, I eventually became a member of the support team looking after *Leander* on its forays on the main line, and being part of that team certainly taught me the basics of working with steam, as nearly all of them were former BR steam footplatemen.

As 1983 was drawing to a close, *Leander* was sold to the Severn Valley Railway, a move which eventually led to the curtailment of its mainline activities with its final run taking place in 1986. Within the following two years an opportunity arose to join a group which was to start the overhaul of former LMS pacific, 46203 *Princess Margaret Rose*. This locomotive, which was based at Butterley in Derbyshire, had been acquired by Brell Ewart who was leading the project to return the engine back into main line running condition. My association with Brell was to last many years, and together with others, we went on to form the Princess Royal Class Locomotive Trust (PRCLT), custodian of locomotives 46203, and two former BR Standard tanks 80080 and 80098; Coronation pacific No. 46233 *Duchess of Sutherland* was to join the pool some years later. I think it is fair to say that from humble beginnings, PRCLT rapidly became one of the leaders in the steam preservation movement, an unbiased view based on the fact that such a small group was able to return no fewer than four steam locomotives to the main line in addition to running its own successful tour company, PMR Tours. During my time with the PRCLT I held several management positions which culminated in the role of Vice-Chairman. One of the obstacles I faced by living in Carlisle however was the regular travelling to Butterley which involved a round trip of more than 400 miles, and it was a journey I was to undertake for more years than I care to remember, sometimes being completed on a day return.

Once *Princess Margaret Rose* was certified for use on the main line in 1990, it was only a matter of time before

Stanier class 5X No. 45690 *Leander* was built at Crewe Works in 1936 and was initially allocated to Crewe North before being transferred to Bristol Barrow Road shed in 1947. The locomotive remained at Barrow Road until it was withdrawn from service in 1964 from where it was dispatched that same year to Messrs Woodham's scrap-yard at Barry, South Wales. After languishing there for eight years, *Leander* was purchased by a Stockport based engineering company with a view to returning the locomotive to traffic on the main line. The photograph, taken on the 6th August 1968, shows to good effect what certain groups were faced with when purchasing a locomotive from Woodhams, as the 5X had by this time, spent four years exposed to the elements at Barry. Photo: Ken Armstrong

Leander's transformation from a Barry wreck was certainly not typical of what most preservationists had to endure to return their locomotive to steam, as the new owners of 5690 arranged for the 5X to be put through BR's Derby works for a major overhaul which saw it return to main line action in 1973. Its maiden run on the S&C took place on the 26th April 1980 with a charter organised by the Leander Locomotive Ltd, from Hellifield to Carlisle and return; the locomotive is pictured approaching Armathwaite with the southbound working. Photo: Ken Armstrong

The splendour of a the S&C is clearly demonstrated in this view looking across to one of the most elegant viaducts on the line as Coronation pacific 46229 *Duchess of Hamilton* crosses Arten Gill Viaduct with a southbound fourteen coach Cumbrian Mountain Express on 9th June 1984.

the S&C would beckon, and the inaugural run on the route took place in June the following year. After that, the locomotive became a regular performer on the line and whilst working with experienced Carlisle based BR crews, I was relentlessly schooled in the art of firing and was often handed the shovel on the heavily graded S&C. This sideline took a somewhat serious turn when I was officially passed-out as a main line fireman by Bill Andrew, the then BR Chief Traction Inspector at Crewe. Considering that I had never worked for British Railways, I was taken aback somewhat by this qualification but I was also pleased, that above all else, I had gained the respect of such eminent railwaymen.

During the years that I was involved with steam on the S&C, I always carried a camera which enabled me to take advantage of the many opportunities to capture behind the scene images, and those, together with material obtained by way of a locally issued lineside photographic permit, feature strongly within the book.

Although *Princess Margaret Rose* understandably features more than others, I have tried to give a balanced view of preserved steam activity on the S&C and in doing so; all forty-eight locomotives are featured.

In addition to explaining how steam returned to the S&C, I have also taken the opportunity to include two purely pictorial chapters which have both been arranged in near date order to accurately record how steam has been operated on the line since 1978. I would like to take this opportunity to thank those photographers who have generously allowed access to their collections; their images contained in the book have been credited accordingly, and to Dick Hardy and Mike Notley for their valued contributions.

This book takes a detailed look at steam operations on the S&C since its triumphant return in 1978 that led to three decades of activity that certainly hasn't been short of colour. We have witnessed representatives of the 'Big Four' tackle the grades, some of which have displayed their attractive pre-nationalised liveries, whilst others have sported colours more connected with the British Railways era. Locomotives to appear have ranged from Compound to Coronation, the humble J36 0-6-0 class to the world record holder *Mallard*, not to mention King, Castle and Merchant Navy. In addition to all of this, we have seen steam locomotives in charge of a genuine local passenger train, a timetabled goods train, and to top it all, the Royal Train.

Howard Routledge, Carlisle. November 2009

Before we take a look at how the steam locomotive returned to the S&C in 1978, we should really start with how it all ended some ten years earlier. The final main-line steam-hauled train ran by British Railways was the infamous 1T57 which departed from Liverpool Lime Street on the 11th August 1968 for its epic journey to Carlisle and return. The route was via Manchester, Blackburn and Hellifield, then the S&C. Although the previous week-end had been the official end for steam, train reporting number 1T57 was billed as a commemorative farewell to the steam locomotive on the national rail network. Britannia class No. 70013 *Oliver Cromwell* had been retained by BR for the numerous 'end of steam' specials that took place during the final weeks, and was therefore an obvious candidate to be involved with the last ever main-line steam-hauled train. Having been allocated the Manchester Victoria to Carlisle leg, 70013 is seen (above right) hauling the train away from Ribblehead Viaduct, whilst another photographer situated nearby, has captured the train's progression towards Blea Moor signal box. Both images give a good indication as to the crowds that gathered near to the lineside that day to witness this most historic event.

Photos: Ken Armstrong (right top) & David S. Goodfellow (right bottom).

Chapter One — 'They Think It's All Over'

Unprecedented scenes at Ais Gill summit as 1T57 stops for a 'photo call' allowing *Oliver Cromwell* to accept the acclaim from the crowd vying for position to get as close as possible to the locomotive. A number of step ladders can be seen having been placed beneath coach doors to allow passengers access to the trackside. It is interesting to note that the crowd isn't wholly made up of steam enthusiasts, as women, young children, and even dogs can be seen in attendance. The often used phrase 'the lonely Ais Gill signal box' certainly didn't apply on 11th August 1968. Photos: Martin Welch (both)

The running of 1T57 involved the use of three Black Five class locomotives, and the return working from Carlisle to Manchester featured a double-headed combination of Nos. 44871 and 44781, seen here passing Kirkby Stephen. Once this train had passed, many at the lineside thought that they had seen the last steam locomotives ever to run on the S&C, but following a short distance behind the train was 70013 *Oliver Cromwell*, running back from Carlisle on part of her journey to her new home at the Bressingham Steam Museum in Norfolk. Photo: Martin Welch

70013 approaches Ais Gill summit, on what could have been described as a fateful journey, but forty years to the day, she was back on the line, once again at the head of 1T57. Photo Ken Armstrong

A unique photograph taken from an elevated position records *Oliver Cromwell* entering Carlisle Citadel station, whilst close examination of the distant West Coast Main Line, reveals the two Black Five locomotives, 44871 and 44781, awaiting signals from No. 5 box which will allow them to back down to the station to couple-up to 1T57 before returning the train back over the S&C. Photo: courtesy Cumberland News

1T57 may have been the end for the British Railways standard gauge steam fleet, but it certainly wasn't the end for steam on the main line. Those who witnessed the events surrounding 1T57 on the S&C could be forgiven for thinking that they had seen the end of steam on the line, but this theory lasted only a mere eleven weeks. On the 26th October 1968, former LNER class A3 No. 4472 *Flying Scotsman* hauled an RCTS special train between Liverpool and Carlisle and once again the route chosen was to include the former Midland line. Coupled to its second tender, 4472 is pictured storming through Kirkby Stephen with the return working (northbound was via Shap). After the events surrounding 1T57, *Flying Scotsman* was the only steam locomotive then allowed access to the national rail network, but this was to last only until 1969 when the locomotive left the country for its ill-fated tour of America. British Railways was then in a position to apply its infamous steam ban. Photo: Martin Welch

Chapter Two — The Return of Steam

Once 1T57 had cleared Settle Junction on the run back to Liverpool, BR seem to have wasted little time with their plan to run down the S&C even long before they finally admitted that their intention was to close the line completely.

Within two years, no fewer than twelve stations had been closed leaving only the two principal stations, Settle and Appleby, open to traffic. Such closures soon led to the former station buildings becoming derelict, and this, coupled with the reduction in the maintenance of other structures, gave the impression that the line was beginning to die on its feet. This was non more apparent than at Ribblehead Viaduct when, in 1981, British Rail announced that the ¼ mile long structure was more or less life expired, and due to its rapidly deteriorating condition the viaduct had at best, five years service left, before a costly £6m repair would have to be met.

Sceptics, who thought that the £6m claim was grossly excessive, were now convinced that BR were using Ribblehead Viaduct, the most visual of structures on the S&C, as the excuse they had been looking for to force through closure of the line. As a result of this announcement by BR, an organisation called the Friends of the Settle-Carlisle Line (FoSCL) was formed which would eventually play a major role in the fight to keep the line open.

Although the steam locomotive had returned to a small number of main lines during 1971, BR were steadfast with their decision that the S&C would not be included in such plans, but in 1978 they appear to have had a change of heart and began to market steam-hauled S&C charter trains in conjunction with a body called the Steam Locomotive Operators Association (SLOA), an organisation which consisted of owners and operators of steam locomotives that were approved by BR for use on the main line.

The eagerly anticipated return of steam onto the S&C occurred on 25th March 1978 (Easter Saturday) when 4771 *Green Arrow* left Leeds with the inaugural train bound for Carlisle.

A Skipton crew had charge of this run with 4771, whilst Carlisle men waited impatiently until the Easter Monday to take charge of the locomotive for the first southbound working on the line. Both sets of crews were fully aware of the importance of completing trouble free and successful runs, which they hoped would lead to further steam work for their respective

After a period of ten years, the sound of a steam hauled train is once again heard on the 'Long Drag' as former LNER class V2 No. 4771 *Green Arrow* battles through blizzard conditions at Horton-In-Ribblesdale with the inaugural train on 25th March 1978. Running from Leeds to Carlisle, the locomotive carried the headboard 'The Norfolkman' in recognition of the work undertaken by Bill Harvey in returning *Green Arrow* back to main line running condition. Photo: Martin Welch

After completing a successful climb, *Green Arrow* takes water at Garsdale with the inaugural train. This image gives a good illustration as to how steam operations on the S&C have changed over the thirty years; the water pipe no longer blocks the up road, nor do people associated with the locomotive stand in the four-foot – with or without a high-vis vest. Photo: Martin Welch

depots. They did not disappoint; both charters ran to plan and were a huge success.

Other steam hauled charters were to quickly follow 4771's ground breaking venture, but one that ran on the 13th May that same year, hauled by 92220 *Evening Star*, made the headlines for all of the wrong reasons with the death at Appleby station of Bishop Eric Treacy. Treacy, the master railway photographer, had initially stumbled and fell whilst using the station footbridge then collapsed and died a short time later near to the site of the former cattle dock. To celebrate the life of such an icon, a memorial service was held at Appleby station on 30th September 1978 attended by no fewer than 4,000 people. Two special steam hauled trains, jointly organised by British Rail and the Steam Locomotive Operators Association, ran over the Settle & Carlisle line to the Appleby service. Three locomotives were in operation, 4472 *Flying Scotsman*, 35028 *Clan Line*, and 92220 *Evening Star* which fittingly provided the backdrop to the proceedings.

With the exception of the stations now closed, the S&C had retained a lot of the features common in 1968, the

only major change to steam operations in the preservation era was that of watering the locomotives. With all such steam age facilities having being withdrawn from use, other means had to be employed which ranged from using water hydrants to road tankers, whilst Garsdale had its own unique natural supply. Locomotives were just as familiar to the crews, after all they were still using the vacuum brake, but although now limited to a maximum speed of 60mph, this was to have no detrimental effect on their use on the S&C as the line speed was, and is still limited, to 60mph.

With the return of steam still in its infancy, the 1980s were to become the most turbulent of years insofar as the retention of the S&C was concerned. After a period of constant denials, BR announced in late 1983 their intention to withdraw passenger services from the line which would see the closure of Appleby and Settle stations. To boost BR's case, the Nottingham-Glasgow express workings were diverted away from the route, and intended passengers were left with two trains per day in each direction between Leeds and Carlisle. With no freight traffic to speak of using the line other than the very occasional train running to Warcop, signalmen were now faced with only four passenger trains per day to deal with, a situation that BR's Special Train Unit, in conjunction with SLOA, took advantage of, in so much that they had little problem in securing suitable paths for their steam hauled charter trains.

In addition to the announced withdrawal of passenger traffic, BR had also begun a programme of closing seven of the fourteen surviving signal boxes. The line was now as lean as could be.

To add to the confusion, eight of the previously closed stations were re-opened during 1986, but the case submitted by BR to withdraw passenger services continued. It wasn't until the following year that BR eventually showed their hand by publishing their financial case for closure of the line.

The fight to retain the S&C was a long and drawn out affair which saw a number of organisations joining together in the campaign to prove that BR were attempting to seek closure

NOTICE OF INTENT TO WITHDRAW RAILWAY PASSENGER SERVICES
SECTION 56(7), TRANSPORT ACT 1962

BRITISH RAILWAYS BOARD
PUBLIC NOTICE
TRANSPORT ACT 1962
WITHDRAWAL OF RAILWAY PASSENGER SERVICES

The **LONDON MIDLAND REGION** of British Railways hereby give notice in accordance with Section 56(7) of the Transport Act, 1962 that they propose to discontinue all railway passenger services between Settle Junction and Carlisle (Petteril Bridge Junction) and from the following stations: —

SETTLE
APPLEBY

It appears to the Board that the following alternative services will be available:

Existing Services — By rail:

The passenger service currently operating between Leeds and Carlisle via Settle and Appleby will be diverted via Giggleswick, Carnforth, Oxenholme and Penrith.

Existing Services — By Road:

Ribble-Pennine-Lancaster City Transport Joint Services 580 and 581 between Settle and Lancaster, Hellifield and Skipton.

Ribble Services 620, 621, 623, 624 and 625 between Appleby and Penrith.

Scott's Greys Service 38 between Appleby, Penrith and Carlisle.

Any users of the rail service which it is proposed to discontinue, and any body representing such users, may lodge an objection to the proposal in writing within six weeks of 24th December 1983, i.e. not later than 4th February 1984, addressing the objection to:

    The Secretary,
    **Transport Users's Consultative Committee for the North Western Area,
    Room 308, Royal Exchange,
    Cross Street,
    Manchester M2 7BR.**

        or

    The Secretary,
    **Transport Users' Consultative Committee for the Yorkshire Area,
    Record House,
    Bootham,
    York YO3 7DQ**

If any such objection is lodged, the service cannot be discontinued until the Transport Users' Consultative Committees have considered the objection and reported to the Secretary of State has given his consent to the closure under Section 56(8) of the Transport Act, 1962.

The Committee may hold a meeting to hear objections. Such a meeting will be held in public and any persons who have lodged an objection in writing may also make oral representations to the Committee. The Committee's report will be published.

If no objections are lodged to the proposal, the service will be discontinued on 14th May, 1984.

Let battle commence.

On the 17th December 1983 a special Cumbrian Mountain Express, hauled by 46229 *Duchess of Hamilton*, conveyed a number of dignitaries including County Councillors local to the line, in order for them to highlight the start of the campaign to oppose closure of the S&C.

Eric Martlew, Chairman of Cumbria County Council and future Member of Parliament for Carlisle, speaks to the assembled crowd at Garsdale. Organisers of the event couldn't have wished for a more imposing backdrop.

(Right) This is the actual notice issued by British Railways in December 1983 announcing their intention to withdraw passenger services from the line, and to close the two remaining stations at Appleby and Settle. Unfortunately for BR, the notice was discovered to be defective which forced them to issue another one, and if matters were not bad enough, the second notice was defective as well and also had to be re-issued. Naturally, these delays gave valuable additional time to those groups opposing such plans and their robust campaigns eventually resulted in no fewer than 30,000 formal objections being made against BR's plan to eventually close the line.

of the line through stealth. FoSCL, County Councils and local Members of Parliament were vocal in their objections to closure and it wasn't until 1989 that the fight was eventually won when Secretary of State Paul Channon, announced to Parliament, that Transport Minister Michael Portillo had refused BR's request to close the line. Although the fight against closure had focussed on the plight of those living close to the line, the victory was also keenly appreciated by steam enthusiasts throughout the country. The premier steam route had been saved.

Throughout the period of the lines uncertainty, BR and SLOA were seen to strengthen their partnership even further with increased numbers of charter trains running under the banner of the *Cumbrian Mountain Express*. This was a two-leg affair using two locomotives based at the former steam shed at Carnforth. One locomotive was to work what was known as the bottom leg, from Carnforth to Skipton, where the second locomotive was waiting to haul the charter over the S&C. After this northbound run, the locomotive was stabled at the Carlisle Upperby depot usually for a period of one or two weeks before the next scheduled return working. The Skipton changeover point was soon changed to Hellifield, an arrangement that lasted for many years.

Although the performance of steam locomotives on the line had usually been beyond reproach, elsewhere on the network matters had not been as fortunate. Management at BR were so concerned at some of the incidents involving steam, that in 1986, David Ward, director of Inter City Special Trains, was put in charge of all main line steam hauled charter trains. His brief was to improve the reliability of steam locomotive performance, and if nothing else, Ward instilled a much needed discipline, and introduced a more business like approach to the subject.

SLOA had also beefed up their management at about the same time with the appointment of Dick Hardy as chairman. Hardy was a former professional senior railwayman with a mass of experience in the management of steam locomotives, not to mention his ability to get the best out of people. With his appointment, SLOA attained some serious credibility. But even though Ward and Hardy were true supporters of steam, they were both fully aware that it was now operating in a completely different age as to that left behind in 1968, and that steam's presence on the main line had to be managed accordingly.

With the Michael Portillo reprieve, there seemed a lot more confidence about the S&C. A number of stations previously closed had been bought by individuals intent

The structure used by British Railways to force through closure was non other than Ribblehead Viaduct. One of the arches had received attention in order to cost the work required to bring the viaduct up to standard; the figure of £6m was hotly disputed by those engaged in the fight against closure. 46229 *Duchess of Hamilton* is seen crossing the viaduct with a northbound Cumbrian Mountain Express on 19th October 1985.

The dilapidated condition of Little Salkeld station is all too evident in this scene recorded on 11th July 1987. Having closed to traffic during 1970, the building was subsequently purchased privately and has since been converted into a dwelling house keeping the original external appearance as built by the Midland Railway. Of note is the station notice-board and clock still in situ on the front of the building. It is also worth mentioning the tower seen in the distance, which I climbed in order to capture the images displayed on page 48.

on restoring them into private dwellings, whilst at the same time, FoSCL were pumping finances into various projects including valuable amenities to those stations that remained open. There was certainly a bit of pride being displayed along the route, even hanging baskets began to appear. Steam was also playing its part in portraying the line to its best advantage; the variety of locomotives certainly added to one of the most interesting periods of the lines history. Not even during the locomotive trials held during the 1950s, had representatives of all the 'big four' railway companies been seen tackling the gradients on the S&C, and in addition to this, the world speed record holder *Mallard* even put in a number of appearances during 1988 to commemorate the 50th anniversary of attaining that historic 126mph. But, as pleasing as all that was, Midland historians would no doubt cite the appearance of a Compound as being the absolute highlight of the 80s, when in 1983, the NRM's No. 1000 was paired with an LMS liveried Jubilee for two runs over a snow covered S&C. For a few hours at least, the S&C had been transported back into the 1940s.

As a new decade dawned in 1990, David Ward couldn't be accused of allowing sentimentality to get in the way of making decisions to improve the performance of steam locomotives using the line.

With a number of locomotives having slipped to a stand during the leaf fall season at locations such as Taitlands and Scotby, diesel assistance had usually to be called upon to push the stricken charters onto more favourable stretches of track. This problem had been aggravated by the scarcity of traffic using the line, in conjunction with the use of lightweight service trains, which were incapable of keeping the rail-head clean.

These incidents would invariably cause delays to other traffic, not to mention the financial implications involved with the necessary recovery work. One answer in such circumstances would have been to remove the cause, which is what exactly occurred when Ward put severe restrictions on the operation of steam locomotives on the line during that period; although a blanket ban wasn't strictly imposed, each proposed charter was now given careful consideration before it was allowed to run.

In addition to that, a major change was forced onto the 1991 summer steam programme when locomotives of less than power class 7 were prohibited from the S&C. This decision was taken because some of the lesser power classes had struggled to maintain timings in adverse conditions.

Quite a contrast in station buildings on the S&C some twenty-one years later as the sun sets on a picturesque Kirkby Stephen station on 17th August 2008. The floral displays featured on the platforms led to an entry in the 2007 Britain in Bloom competition which resulted in the station winning the silver award. How times have changed on the former Midland line.

David Ward retired during 1994, and on the 1st April the following year, the railway industry was privatised. To mark the demise of British Railways, a special steam hauled train ran over the S&C from Carlisle to Liverpool on 31st March of that year.

Waterman Railways initially replaced BR Special Trains Unit to become the new partner of SLOA to manage all main line steam activities working through a regulatory train operating company called Rail Express Systems (RES), and although a number of footplate crew had retired, things were running more or less just the same as before. RES would eventually become an arm of freight giant EWS, and although that company were to retain their steam operating safety case, another company was to challenge their monopoly to steam, when West Coast Railways (WCR) from Carnforth also attained that accreditation. Employing a number of re-cently retired steam crews, WCR quickly established itself as a creditable Train Operating Company and soon began to be seen as the dominant operator for steam hauled charter trains.

Throughout all of this, the Settle-Carlisle railway has witnessed a renaissance with a huge increase in traffic using the line. Freight, particularly heavily laden coal trains, has become a common feature to daily activities. In addition to this, massive engineering work has been undertaken to improve both track and structures to ensure that the line is capable of meeting the demands of the 21st century. It is encouraging to report, that amongst all of this, the common steam locomotive can still be seen and heard tackling the 1 in 100 grades to reach the summit at Ais Gill.

Some things just never change.

Chapter Three – Behind The Footplate

The first positive signs Carlisle crews had that steam was to return to the S&C was in early 1978 when Chief Traction Inspector George Gordon pinned a sheet of paper onto the notice board within the signing-on point asking for volunteers to return as steam drivers and firemen. Names soon appeared on that sheet of paper which was eventually to lead to no fewer than twenty-five former Canal, Upperby and Kingmoor men answering the call to form the infamous 'Carlisle steam panel'.

Although a much smaller depot than Carlisle, Skipton also had no problem in securing the services of former steam personnel eager to return to the master craft, and whilst the roster system was to face many changes over the years, the initial working arrangement usually saw Skipton men working the northbound (down) trains, whilst Carlisle crews had charge of the up workings.

Those BR crews were to see several changes to steam workings compared with what they had pre 1968. To begin with, doctors employed by British Rail placed an 80 mile restriction on the distance that firemen could be employed on the shovel, an instruction which led to the majority of S&C steam charters being rostered two firemen with their changeover point usually occurring at the Garsdale water stop. But perhaps the biggest change concerned the actual locomotives as they were all now privately owned and supported by individuals, the majority of whom were not professional railwaymen. In days gone by, when the crew signed-on at a BR steam depot they would have been allocated a locomotive which they would then proceed to prepare for the road. Matters such as ensuring that sufficient coal and water was on board were taken for granted at any steam depot, and whilst the driver commenced to oil-up, the fireman would start to prepare the fire for departure. The introduction of the preserved steam locomotive removed at a stroke all of those previ-

When steam returned to the S&C in 1978, locomotive owners were fortunate that so many experienced men volunteered to return as drivers and firemen at both Carlisle and Skipton depots. Such experience is pictured at Appleby on 23rd February 1985 as Carlisle based BR crews stand in front of former Kingmoor Black Five 44767: (L to R) Gordon Hodgson (Carlisle Canal & Kingmoor), Paul Kane (Kingmoor), Brian Grierson (Kingmoor), Ian Howson (Upperby & Kingmoor) and Jimmy Lister. Jim began his railway career with the LNER at Corstorphine in 1937 before joining the locomotive department at St Margarets shed in Edinburgh two years later. Whilst waiting for a vacancy to become a cleaner, he became aware that such a position was available at Carlisle and he subsequently transferred to the Canal shed in 1940 to begin his footplate career. Upon closure of the Canal in 1963, Jim then moved to the former Caledonian stronghold at Kingmoor.

ously held responsibilities from the BR crew, and were now managed by the owning group who accompanied the locomotive on its runs on the main line. This group became officially known as the 'locomotive support crew'.

The main task of the locomotive support crew was to hand over to a BR crew a fully prepared steam locomotive ready for 'the off'.

The coaling and watering, including the management of the water stops en-route, were the responsibility of the owning group, as was the preparation of the locomotive included oiling up and steam raising etc.

One member of the support team was allowed to remain on the footplate to accompany the crew from BR, and he was officially recognised as being the 'owner's representative'. The representative's qualifications would vary from group to group, but in the particular group of which I was a member, this person had at least to be a qualified fireman and had to possess a full working knowledge of the locomotive's controls. His attendance was also to assist and advise the BR crew on any aspect concerning the

Whilst former LMS class 5 No. 5305 stands on the up main line at Howe & Co Sidings signal box on the 10th May 1986, Chief Traction Inspector Ron Gerrard takes time out whilst awaiting the arrival of the diesel-hauled charter train which 5305 will return south. Ron, a former Carnforth based BR steam man, moved to Carlisle to take up the top footplate position upon the retirement of long-serving George Gordon.

engine. Owing to the presence of this non-BR person on the footplate, a Traction Inspector had to be present at all times, and because of this requirement, Inspectors became a regular feature on all steam hauled charters.

At first, there were no official restrictions as to whom, or how many persons constituted a support crew, but as the years progressed, this situation was to change dramatically. From 1989 onwards, restrictions began to be put in place which eventually required support crew members to fall in line with BR crews in so much, as they had to attain a Personal Track Safety (PTS) certificate; this became a prerequisite for access onto any railway infrastructure. The PTS was renewable every two years, as was the medical that accompanied such qualification. Numbers were restricted to six persons on any team, one member of which was designated the title of Responsible Officer (RO).

The footplate crew, and to a lesser degree, the locomotive support crew, are the ones who operate most in the public eye, but there has always been a very large team working in the background actively supporting steam's continued presence on the main line. Mention has al-

ready been made of the officials at SLOA, whose work in the early days with a somewhat anti-steam lobby at BR, undoubtedly laid the foundations of what we have today. A number of professional railwaymen have also worked alongside SLOA, such as Carlisle based engineer John Duncan who held the post of Chief Mechanical Engineer for many years. In addition to keeping locomotive owners abreast of new working practices etc, it was John that researched and developed the absolute spark arrester device which proved so successful in keeping steam hauled charter trains running through hot summer months when lineside fire-risk conditions were most prevalent.

Another little known but important element to the team involved those individuals tasked with the detailed examinations of locomotive boilers and mechanical components. These examiners were initially time-served BR men but privatisation allowed other parties to become involved with this massive safety critical work.

It was these and other individuals who provided such a high degree of competence which enabled the whole steam package to be acceptable to BR.

Footplate Inspector Jim McClelland and Driver Willie Little pose with Southern Merchant Navy 35028 *Clan Line* at Upperby on the 17th December 1988. Jim started his railway career in 1946 at Newton Stewart, a sub-shed to Stranraer, before transferring to Kingmoor in 1955 where he was passed-out as a driver three years later. When steam returned to the S&C in 1978, he was the driver of the first southbound run which featured *Green Arrow* hauling The Norfolkman from Carlisle to Skipton. Upon his promotion to Traction Inspector, Jim became a regular figure on steam locomotives running on the S&C during the 1980s and 1990s.

To begin with, steam workings on the S&C ran between Carlisle and Leeds, and for Carlisle crews, the southbound charters involved working as far as Skipton where they were relieved by a fresh set of men. These working practices however, were to alter back and forth throughout the years. With the advent of the 'Cumbrian Mountain Express' programme, crews from Carnforth came into the equation in order to work the bottom leg from Carnforth across to either Skipton or Hellifield, where the locomotive changeover for the S&C would take place. As the years progressed however, the southern extremity to the steam leg for S&C charter trains, kept being extended, first of all from Hellifield to Blackburn, then to Farington Junction (wcml south of Preston), and eventually Crewe. Carlisle crews benefited from most of these changes,

Senior officials pose for a group photograph at SLOA's Annual General Meeting on 15th January 1994 and include: (L to R) Brell Ewart, Chairman of SLOA and the Princess Royal Class Locomotive Trust, Bernard Staite, Charter train organiser and former SLOA Secretary, Jim McClelland, Carlisle Footplate Inspector (guest), Dick Hardy, former Chairman of SLOA, Julian Riddick, Chairman A4 Locomotive Society, and David Ward, Director, Inter-City Special Trains Unit.

working to and from either Blackburn or Farington.

The 1991 decision to extend to Farington Junction was a major breakthrough as it meant that steam could hand directly over to electric traction on the WCML. Economically speaking, this was a welcome move, as it negated the costly use of a diesel locomotive over the short section of line between Blackburn and Farington.

With one eye on the future, David Ward decided that a training programme would be held on the S&C in early 1993 to pass-out additional steam crews based at the Carlisle depot. The locomotive used was Standard class 4 tank No. 80080 which completed two round trips daily from Carlisle to Kirkby Stephen with a four coach train. Stops were made at all of the intermediate stations, which meant that for the first time since 1966, a steam hauled local passenger train was to be seen on the line. This three week programme allowed five long-serving firemen to qualify as steam drivers.

It probably came as little surprise, when in that same year, David Ward decided that all steam work on the line should be allocated to the Carlisle depot. In an effort to make train crew operation more efficient, basing the steam locomotives at Carlisle would allow one set of men, with a spare fireman, to work Carlisle to Farington Junction and return light engine, (or vice versa). To implement this, no fewer than five pacifics were based at Carlisle Upperby for the summer season. The only thing that was missing was the roundhouse!

The final extension to steam mileage was authorised from December 1994 when Crewe became the new locomotive changeover point. Authority to run under the wires from Crewe to Farington now gave passengers 160 miles of steam haulage through to Carlisle. Footplate staff from Crewe had now joined the team and they worked as far as Blackburn, being relieved there by Carlisle men for the run over the S&C.

Although the crewing arrangements didn't appear to alter after privatisation of the railway industry in 1995, what was noticeable was the number of retirements that had taken place. Freight company EWS, the main provider of steam crews, was left with a handful of men based at Carlisle and they were occasionally forced to 'ship-in' firemen from other depots.

With the oncoming of West Coast Railways however, the roster altered once more with one set of men working throughout between Crewe and Carlisle.

In conclusion, it seems appropriate to mark the passage of time concerning the footplate roster and to highlight the situation prevailing in a once proud railway city like Carlisle. In the 1960s, Carlisle still boasted having three steam depots employing probably in excess of 2,000 footplate staff, and then went on to play a major role in returning steam to the S&C. It now has only one ex-BR steam man left on its books.

When Brian Grierson started his railway career as a cleaner at Kingmoor during 1964, he couldn't possibly have envisaged that he would eventually become the last man to appear on a Carlisle steam related roster board.

He no doubt would be the first to agree that the rostering of steam crews has been a story all of it's own during the thirty years since George Gordon simply pinned that sheet of paper onto the notice-board.

Having being involved with steam's return to the main line in 1971, Bernard Staite became Secretary to the newly formed Steam Locomotive Operators Association in 1975. In addition to representing the interests of steam locomotive owners, SLOA was in partnership with British Railways in the running of main line steam-hauled charter trains, and Bernard, who was the SLOA representative in organising such trains, was also the train manager on the day of the run. When BR decided in 1978 to include the S&C as a steam approved route, Bernard began to market trains on the line such as the highly successful Cumbrian Mountain Express. David Ward estimates that in the years 1980-89 at least 300 such trains ran over the S&C conveying well over 100,000 passengers; and in one particular year alone, a staggering 44 Cumbrian Mountain Express trains ran. When Secretary of State Paul Channon announced to Parliament in 1989 that BR's application to close the route was being refused, he made mention that revenue from the line had risen within the previous 12 months by an astounding 40%. I wonder how many charter trains organised by Bernard contributed to that figure, not to mention Transport Minister Michael Portillo's decision to refuse closure.
Bernard Staite is pictured speaking at York on the 20th April 1994 prior to an A4 hauled run over the S&C to mark the retirement of David Ward.

Sunday 9th July 1989 saw LNER class K4 No. 3442 *The Great Marquess* haul a train from Manchester to Carlisle, a positioning run used to get the locomotive to Fort William. This had been the engine's first run over the S&C, and as usual with such events, there is quite a sizable support crew. The BR crew are seen posing with the Severn Valley Railway based support team for a group photograph shortly after arrival at the Carlisle Upperby depot.

Princess Royal class No. 46203 *Princess Margaret Rose* takes water at Long Preston on 6th July 1991 whilst en route from Carlisle with what appears to be a diverted up Royal Scot. Standing next to the locomotive amongst members of the BR and support crews, is Dick Hardy, the then chairman of the Steam Locomotive Operators Association (SLOA).

LNER Class A3 No. 4472 *Flying Scotsman* pauses at Garsdale with a northbound charter train in order to replenish her tender tank. Under normal circumstances, the support crew handle such stops for water - by laying out the hoses etc, but Garsdale was always that bit different due to a certain individual by the name of Bill Allan, i/c Garsdale water. Bill, seen wearing his S&C weather-beaten sun hat, is pictured on top of the A3's tender; and was for many years, responsible for maintaining the water supply at Garsdale until its demise during 2003, when he promptly transferred his services to Appleby. Photo: Gordon Hodgson

A long way from servicing an engine on the Cumbrian Mountain Express, but this is the other side of life within a support crew as we see *Princess Margaret Rose* during her 21 month major overhaul which was carried out at the Midland Railway Centre, Butterley. This view, recorded on the 25th November 1989, shows the tender being lifted by the centre's 50 ton steam breakdown crane in order for it to be re-united with the tender-chassis. Work to the locomotive's boiler was also well advanced by this time, and although steaming was only a matter of 6 month's away, the S&C would have to wait an additional 12 months before 46203 would make her first appearance on the 'Long Drag'.

Initially, steam locomotives that operated on the main line were examined every six months with regard to their mechanical and boiler condition; the safety critical nature of such examinations obviously cannot be overstated.

Whilst these tasks were still the responsibility of British Railways, such examinations were carried out by these two time-served officials, Brian Penny (left) and Sam Foster, seen here during an 'in-steam' exam on *Princess Margaret Rose* on 17th March 1994 prior to a Derby – Carlisle run the following day. Long serving 46203 support crew member John Riley looks on.

The six monthly examinations were split up into two, a 'cold' exam, (locomotive not in steam) and a 'steam' exam (locomotive in steam). The cold exam allowed the boiler examiner, Sam Foster (pictured), access into the smokebox and firebox, and also to view the water space surrounding the inner firebox by using a small mirror which he is seen placing through one of the wash-out plug holes.

The 'steam' exam would normally be held a few days later, and here we see Sam Foster, firing shovel in hand, and careful observation will reveal that a stainless steel plate has been attached to the shovel so that it acts as a mirror. This allowed an examination of the interior of the firebox whilst the locomotive was being maintained at full steam pressure.

In addition to the six monthly examinations, steam locomotives were also inspected prior to each run on the main line and here we see BR examiner Dick Armstrong in the process of opening the smokebox door on *Duchess of Hamilton* whilst he carries out a Fitness to Run (FTR) inspection at Upperby on the 10th August 1993.

The loss of experienced footplate staff was keenly felt in the weeks leading up to privatisation of the railways. On 19th March 1994, Driver David Gardner (centre) and Footplate Inspector Jim McClelland (right) jointly called a day to nearly 100 years railway service when they worked former LMS pacific 46203 *Princess Margaret Rose* on a southbound Cumbrian Mountain Express. After working with them for many years, it was a sad sight to see both climb down from the footplate for the final time opposite Leeds Holbeck shed. Completing the picture, which was taken prior to departure from Upperby, is a young fireman with a mere 42 years of experience, Paul Kane.

(Previous page, lower) It is not everyone who is fortunate enough to have a steam locomotive named after them, even if it is only for a day, but that is what exactly happened when David Ward called time on his railway career and retired from the position of Director, BR Inter City Special Trains Unit. To mark his retirement, staff from the unit arranged a special charter train, hauled by David's favourite class of locomotive, an LNER A4 pacific (No. 4498) on 20th April 1994 for a run from York to Carlisle via the S&C. Whilst on the former Midland line, the opportunity was offered to David to occupy a privileged position on the footplate under the very close supervision of Driver Jackie Eden. Jack's claim to fame was that he was the last member of staff at Kingmoor to be passed out as a driver prior to the closure of the shed in 1967. The fireman for this special occasion was non other than Dick Hardy.

Near to the end of the British Railways era, and for the first few years of the privatised railway, a good number of experienced steam crew retired from the industry. This undoubtedly caused concern with many preserved steam groups but non more so than the PRCLT who were due to return a Princess Coronation – 6233 *Duchess of Sutherland* - to the main line in 2001. If ever a class of locomotive required experienced crews, this was it; even BR had placed restrictions as to which footplate grades could man such locomotives in normal steam days. Fortunately, a number of recently retired men had joined West Coast Railways (WCR) at Carnforth and it was to that company that we turned to for them to become the Train Operating Company (TOC) for our tour arm – PMR Tours. In addition to supplying footplate crews/guards and coaching stock, they would also liaise on our behalf with Railtrack/Network Rail to implement our tour proposals.

One such experienced footplateman who gravitated to Carnforth was Frank Santrian. Frank (pictured) had begun his steam apprenticeship at Stoke in 1950 before moving to Crewe where he became a regular figure on preserved steam locomotives working out of the Cheshire town. After his retirement from EWS in 1999, Frank joined the staff at West Coast and although no stranger to working the Cumbrian Mountain Express charters between Crewe and Blackburn, once he joined WCR the S&C was soon added to his route knowledge.

The other half of the WCR double act, Bill Andrew, is pictured with the author on 6233 *Duchess of Sutherland* on the 19th April 2003. Bill had come through the steam links at Crewe North shed and eventually rose to the position of Chief Traction Inspector. I had first met Bill whilst working out of Crewe with 46203, but he began to appear on S&C steam workings from approximately 1993 onwards. After retirement from EWS, Bill also joined West Coast Railways, to continue his footplate career, in addition to becoming their Operations Manager. Photo: Peter Fitton

The following pages highlight the role played by three depots that have been used at one time or another to service and stable steam locomotives involved with S&C workings. We begin with a panoramic view of Carlisle Upperby, a former LNWR depot that was used by all preserved steam locomotives working into Carlisle from 1978 until the demise of British Railways in March 1995. From that date, the depot eventually came under the control of EWS who introduced certain restrictions as to who could use the facilities. Two outside pit roads were made available for steam locomotives visiting the depot. The brick built building to the left of the pit roads was a multi-road carriage maintenance shed and was usually off-limits as far as steam locomotives were concerned. The West Coast Main Line can be seen in the far distance.

One point of interest is the area of land to the right of the motor car, upon which stood the 32 road concrete built roundhouse of which I still have vivid memories of visiting on most Sundays during the early 1960s when it would be full of former LMS passenger class locomotives.

A3 4472 *Flying Scotsman* can be seen on one of the pit roads whilst being prepared for its next call to duty on the 17th June 1983.

Another former BR depot involved with steam's presence on the S&C was Carnforth. Unlike Upperby which remained as a working BR depot post 1968, Carnforth shed had been privately purchased after its closure by BR and was opened to the public. Operating under the name of Steamtown, enthusiasts were able to visit a virtual working steam shed which still housed all of the facilities common with a BR steam depot. As a result of this, Carnforth was extremely popular in the early days of the Cumbrian Mountain Express when visitors to the shed were able to see the two locomotives being prepared for duty that day. When the shed was later purchased by David Smith, the site became the operating/engineering centre of the West Coast Railway Co. and was subsequently closed to public access. As it happened, the centre's role in the preparation etc of steam locomotives on CME duty had diminished somewhat, mainly because of the introduction of S&C steam workings being extended south of Hellifield. Stanier 4-6-0s Nos. 5690 *Leander* and 5407 are pictured at Carnforth on the morning of the 11th May 1985 with the coaling and ash plant towers dominating the scene.

With the loss of the facilities at Upperby to those groups working with a TOC other than EWS, the usual practice was then to work in and out of Carlisle on the same day, but after one particular northbound run over the S&C, I was keen for 6233 to remain in the north-west before its next run south some days later. A request to stable the locomotive at Carnforth was greeted favourably, so after hauling a Crewe to Carlisle charter via the S&C on the 29th June 2002, *Duchess of Sutherland* then ran along the WCML to the former 24L shed to await her next duty. This is the scene at Carnforth on Thursday 11th July prior to preparing 6233 for its next run 2 days later, which obviously entailed returning to Carlisle in order to pick up the charter from there.

Once the decision had been made to extend the S&C steam leg as far south as Crewe, Crewe Heritage Centre then began to be utilised to cater for the locomotives working over the former Midland line. Situated immediately north of the station, the centre had been built on the former site of Crewe Works and it is therefore most appropriate that three of Stanier's finest are shown there on the 11th April 1993: 46203 *Princess Margaret Rose*, 6201 *Princess Elizabeth* and 46229 *Duchess of Hamilton*.

I always enjoyed my time at Crewe, the staff there were always helpful and very friendly, but more importantly from a support crew point of view, its biggest plus factor was that it had a supermarket next door. When you are operating away from your home for a few days, such things like that suddenly become very important. The only downside at the centre was the amenity facility which consisted of a one room cabin which contained a shower, a wash hand basin and a toilet. Taking a shower was always a risky business; the slightest movement and the three-sided curtain would come crashing down. It is difficult to say who got the biggest shock when this happened, the person in the shower, or anyone brave enough to be sat on the nearby toilet.

Chapter Four – **Thirty Colourful Years.**

After returning steam to the S&C on 25th March 1978, LNER class V2 No. 4771 *Green Arrow* had charge of the return charter two days later and is pictured here storming towards the summit at Ais Gill. As already mentioned in the previous chapter, the driver on this historic occasion was Jim McClelland, whilst the firemen were Derek Smith and my brother, Geoff Routledge. Photo: Peter Fitton

After the successful runs with *Green Arrow*, further steam hauled charter trains were to appear on the line within the following weeks, the first of those being the 'Border Venturer' which featured Standard class No. 92220 *Evening Star* between Hellifield - Carlisle and return on 13th May 1978. 92220, the last steam locomotive to be built by British Railways, is seen approaching Newbiggin with the southbound working. It was whilst photographing this locomotive a short time later at Appleby that Eric Treacy died. Photo: Peter Fitton

LNER class A3 No. 4472 *Flying Scotsman* made its return to the S&C on 16th June 1978 with a special charter train organised by the locomotive's owner, Sir William McAlpine. Whilst the support crew busy themselves on top of the locomotive's tender (top), a group of young school children seem to be enjoying a visit to the line to witness the presence of 4472. Photo: Peter Fitton

The perils of taking water on the down road at Garsdale are all too apparent as an official keeps a watchful eye on a diesel-hauled goods train that has been halted at signals (bottom). Photo: Martin Welch

The memorial service held at Appleby on 30th September 1978 to celebrate the life of Bishop Eric Treacy featured two steam-hauled charter trains titled 'The Lord Bishop' and 'The Bishop Treacy' which were worked north to the event by Class A3 4472 *Flying Scotsman* and Class 9F 92220 *Evening Star*. The A3 is seen nearing Appleby at Great Ormside. Merchant Navy Class No. 35028 *Clan Line* later returned one of the charters south from Carlisle. Photo: Peter Fitton

A Garter Blue liveried A4 pacific, 4498 *Sir Nigel Gresley*, races by Duncowfold, some 5 miles south of Carlisle, with an up Cumbrian Mountain Express. Although there is a clear blue sky, the prominent exhaust gives the impression that the photograph could well have been recorded on a day when the temperature has been a touch cooler than what it appears. Photo: Ken Armstrong

A snow covered S&C welcomes Stanier Black 5 No. 5305 to Ais Gill summit on the 22nd March 1980. The photograph has been taken from the signal box which at that time was in its final year of service before being saved by preservationists and moved to the Midland Railway Centre at Butterley, Derbyshire. The number of passengers seen braving the elements in order to saviour the delights of a steam-hauled charter train climbing to the summit demonstrates the enthusiast customer base prevalent at that time; it is certainly not the case with today's steam charter traffic. Photo: Peter Fitton

A3 class 4472 *Flying Scotsman* powers a northbound charter across the Ribble Bridge on the 12th April 1980. Officially known as Bridge No. 28, it is located immediately north of Sherrif Brow Viaduct, both structures of which allow the railway to cross the River Ribble twice within a very short distance. Photo: Peter Fitton

On the 17th April 1980 the S&C witnessed a most unusual event as former North British 0-6-0 goods engine No. 673 *Maude* traversed the line on its way to the Rainhill Trials 150 Anniversary celebrations. Because of the tinder dry conditions prevailing at that time, management within BR instructed that a number of steam locomotives had to be diesel hauled to the event, but the owners of 673 were adamant that their locomotive would only attend if it made its own way there. Whilst the locomotive was taking water at Appleby however, a decision was taken to err on the side of caution and to fit a temporary spark arrester for the climb to the summit. In scenes that are reminiscent of the 'Titfield Thunderbolt' where the townsfolk turn up to see what has befallen their engine, we see the smokebox being emptied of ash whilst someone else is forming an emergency spark-arrester with what appears to be nothing more than a roll of chicken-wire. When the journey resumed from Appleby, such was the impairment to the locomotive's steaming ability, the spark-arrester was discarded within 5 miles at Griseburn. Photos: Gordon Hodgson (both)

Built by the North British Railway Company in 1891 as Class C No. 673, the locomotive had served in France during the First World War prior to coming under the ownership of the LNER and reclassified as a J36. Re-numbered 65243 by BR, *Maude* completed no fewer than 75 years service before being withdrawn in 1966 prior to being purchased by the Scottish Railway Preservation Society. Allocated to the Edinburgh area for most of her service, I came across *Maude* during a visit to Haymarket shed in 1963 when the locomotive was one of only four steam engines present, and again in 1966 when it was languishing at the back of Bathgate depot. Whilst *Maude's* southbound run on the S&C was blessed with sunny weather, its return north on the 31st May 1980 was unfortunately accompanied by rain which is quite evident in this view of the locomotive as it passes Ais Gill signal box. Photo: Peter Fitton

A brief pause at Garsdale (below) allows the support crew to replenish the tender by way of the pipe seen obstructing the up road. This unconventional method was only eradicated when the necessary pipe-work was installed under the tracks. Photo: Martin Welch

Leander's second visit to the line took place on the 21st August 1980 and it certainly wasn't short of drama. Heading a southbound CME, 5690's progression towards the summit was halted by the signalman at Kirkby Stephen who informed the footplate staff that a Class 40 hauled goods had failed on the up line on the approach to Garsdale. *Leander* was detached from her train before running wrong line to Garsdale in order to then set back onto the stricken diesel (40179). This famous rescue is seen crossing Moorcock Viaduct before the goods train was deposited in the Garsdale sidings from where *Leander* returned to Kirkby Stephen in order to resume her journey towards Skipton. Photo: Chris Milner

Southern class N15 No. 777 *Sir Lamiel* made its first appearance on the S&C on the 27th March 1982 whilst double-heading a Cumbrian Mountain Pullman. Concerns regarding the capability of the King Arthur to haul a heavy train on the steeply graded line resulted with the addition of 5407 as suitable insurance, an arrangement that was also employed on the return working the following week.

After climbing at 1 in 100 from Settle Junction, the pair are pictured approaching the half-way point of the 15 mile incline which ends just inside the southern portal of Blea Moor tunnel. The train includes eight Pullman cars which had been purchased by SLOA and were used top and tailed with two brake composite (BCK) vehicles; the set had first appeared on the line during May 1981. Photo: Peter Fitton

Class K1 No. 2005 heads an 11 coach Northumbrian Mountain Pullman at Ormside Viaduct on the 22nd January 1983. After departure from Appleby, the locomotive has covered some 2 miles towards Ormside from where the climb really begins, at mostly 1 in 100, for fifteen miles to the summit at Ais Gill. As a result of losing time between Carlisle and Hellifield due to shortage of steam, the Driver and Footplate Inspector had both asserted that the locomotive was overloaded with 11 carriages. This concern had generated some discussion as to the engine's power classification which later resulted in an instruction being issued that restricted the locomotive to 9 vehicles on future work on the line.

Of note is SLOA's Pullman set which is seen with a number of the vehicles having been re-painted into the more customary Pullman livery. Photo: Peter Fitton

When preserved steam locomotives began to appear on the line from 1978 onwards, the National Railway Museum was undoubtedly the largest owning supplier. Whilst *Green Arrow*, *Evening Star*, *Duchess of Hamilton* and the Midland Compound all emanated from the York museum, other locomotives from the national collection, but operated by outside bodies, also put in appearances. One such engine was former Southern 4-6-0 No. 850 *Lord Nelson* pictured here with a southbound charter at Duncowfold, near Cotehill. Photo: Ken Armstrong

The classic combination of a Midland Compound and an LMS liveried Jubilee appeared on the S&C on 5th February 1983 when Nos. 1000 and 5690 *Leander* hauled a northbound charter to Carlisle. The run was marred by late running, not to mention the blizzard conditions that prevailed on the higher ground. The pair returned the southbound Cumbrian Mountain Pullman the following Saturday and with the Compound being deemed too high to go under the overhead wires at Carlisle, the locomotive exchanges were carried out at Howe & Co Sidings signal box. Whilst at Appleby, the opportunity was taken for the crews to swop footplates in order for all of them to sample the delights of working on a Compound, and with Driver David Tibbetts now at the controls of the NRM's veteran, the train is seen on the final approach towards Ais Gill summit. The bottom image shows the pair departing Garsdale after the customary water-stop.

I had visited Upperby the previous day to see both locomotives being prepared, a visit that eventually led to me joining the support crew of 5690, an association with mainline steam that was to last for 21 years.

It is difficult to comprehend that such crowd scenes were allowed on the running line as late as 1983 - even on the S&C, but this remarkable picture shows 46229 *Duchess of Hamilton* at a photographic stop held at Dent on 29th October that year. Photo: Martin Welch

Once on the move from Dent, *Duchess of Hamilton* makes progress through stunning afternoon light as it clears Moorcock Viaduct with the northbound Cumbrian Mountain Express. The magnificent support coach seen behind the locomotive is an LNW clerestory brake compartment from the Edwardian Royal Train, whilst the three coaches seen immediately behind, form the '55 Dining Club', a David Jenkinson initiative which offered on-board prepared meals served Pullman style to your seat. Photo: Martin Welch

Southern West Country No. 34092 *City of Wells* joins the northern end of the S&C at Petteril Bridge Junction on 31st August 1985 with a 12 coach Cumbrian Mountain Pullman.

After stopping at Garsdale for water, Stanier Class 5 No. 5305 is seen crossing Moorcock Viaduct as it heads north towards Ais Gill on the 8th March 1986.

Jubilee No. 5593 *Kolhapur* made a welcome return to the S&C on the 21st March 1987, and is pictured tackling the grade at Helwith Bridge with a Cumbrian Mountain Express. 5593 became a Leeds Holbeck engine during 1965, and it regularly worked over the line until withdrawal from service in October 1967, when she was then purchased for preservation direct from BR. Unfortunately, *Kolhapur*'s 1987 visit to the S&C hasn't been repeated. Photo: Peter Fitton

Another view of the area surrounding Helwith Bridge shows 6201 *Princess Elizabeth* powering a northbound 'Euston 150' celebration train on the 25th July 1987. The Princess Royal pacific, which had taken over the train at Blackburn, certainly creates an impressive sight with what appears to be a recently painted all-maroon coach set. Photo: Peter Fitton

Flying Scotsman passes through Little Salkeld station with a Carlisle to York express on 4th July 1987. This aerial view gives a good indication of a typical rural station that the Midland Railway built along the S&C and shows the former station master's house, and a pair of terraced houses which would have been occupied by other railway workers connected with that area. To obtain these images, I was given permission by a factory manager to climb to the top of the water tank tower - as shown on page 21. Once at the top of the tower, I discovered that the tank was full of water but was relieved to see that it was covered. Unfortunately, the cover was made out of corrugated iron sheets which tended to bounce a little in response to the slightest movement. Having secured a near stable position, the A3 then came into view with the pre-arranged black smoke courtesy of fireman John Finlinson. The going-away shot sees 4472 crossing Dodds Mill Viaduct as it heads towards Langwathby. What Driver Willie Alexander and Inspector Jim McClelland thought as they looked upwards is best left to one's imagination.

BR Standard class 9F No 92220 *Evening Star*, the last steam locomotive to be built by British Railways, emerged from Swindon Works in March 1960. The locomotive saw only 5 years service with BR and upon its withdrawal from Cardiff East Dock shed, it was subsequently donated to the National Collection and ultimately came under the stewardship of the National Railway Museum at York. After being returned to main line service by the NRM, 92220 began to appear on the S&C from 1978, but it had what could be best described as a sporadic existence on the main line due to issues involving the locomotive's flangeless centre driving wheels allegedly conflicting with raised check rails.

During a period when a set of Carlisle men relieved Skipton crews at Appleby, *Evening Star* is pictured with what is believed to be one of its final appearances on the S&C on 16th April 1988 and is seen (above) on one of the two holding roads behind Appleby North signal box awaiting the passage of a down service train. Fireman John Finlinson appears to be keeping a watch for the passage of that train which will herald the commencement of a propelling movement which will demonstrate how railwaymen from a number of different grades work together as a single unit to ensure that such a move is undertaken with upmost safety. The bottom image highlights the problem that faced Driver Duncan McPherson as he is still acting 'blind' whilst he approaches the final stage of the manoeuvre with his 13 coach train.

The final image (overleaf) shows 92220 in heavy rain as it departs Appleby for Carlisle on the final leg of that day's Cumbrian Mountain Express.

On 14th May 1988, the Cambridge Railway Society organised a charter train from Cambridge to Carlisle in order to sample a steam hauled run over the S&C with A4 pacific 4498 *Sir Nigel Gresley*. The northbound working was diesel hauled but unfortunately it was reported as running very late. The A4, which was to work the train from Carlisle to York, was dispatched to Howe & Co Sidings signal box, some 4 miles south of Carlisle, where the locomotive changeover was re-arranged to take place in an effort to recover some of the lost time. Here we see footplate Inspector Jim McClelland in Howe's box where he is being updated to the fact that the charter had been a staggering 90 minutes late at Doncaster. In view of this, the A4 then proceeded to Appleby to complete the changeover there.

After climbing for 3 miles at 1 in 132 from Petteril Bridge Junction, 4498 *Sir Nigel Gresley* runs onto level track as it makes its approach towards Howe & Co Sidings signal box on 18th June 1988. The severity of the incline is amply demonstrated by the position of the distant road bridge at Cumwhinton, but the respite is only for one mile, and then it's back to 1 in 132. The beauty of the S&C!

Stanier class 8F No. 48151 clears Drybeck Viaduct, near Armathwaite, on the 25th June 1988 with a Leeds to Carlisle and return working. Although the locomotive featured on the line pre 1968, this was its first visit since it had returned to the main line in 1987.

To celebrate the 50th anniversary of setting the world speed record, the NRM allowed 4468 *Mallard* some time out of the museum in order to complete a number of main line runs, four of which took place on the S&C in July and August 1988. The locomotive is seen emerging from a steam-filled London Road bridge in Carlisle as it makes steady progress towards Petteril Bridge Junction.

The year 1988 was certainly one for the Garter Blue livery as 4498 *Sir Nigel Gresley* features once again on the line as it passes Howe & Co Sidings signal box on the 27th July with a northbound mid-week Pennine Limited.

Mallard, the world speed record holder, suffers the indignity of stopping for a 'blow-up' at Birkett Common on its final appearance on the S&C on the 27th August 1988. One can only assume that matters must have been quite bad on the footplate as the photographer had ample time to return to his car parked some distance away on Tommy Road before driving to Ais Gill from where he observed the A4 pass under more favourable conditions.   Photo: Peter Fitton

The picturesque Eden Valley plays host to Paddy Smith's Stanier Black Five No. 5407, seen heading north through Baron Wood on 7th September 1988 with the Pennine Limited.

A shot taken from the comfort of Howe & Co Sidings signal box on 6th May 1989 as 4771 *Green Arrow* runs under clear signals on its descent towards Citadel station with a down express.

During 1989, LNER class K4 No. 3442 *The Great Marquess* made a brief appearance on the Fort William-Mallaig line but whilst the Severn Valley Railway based locomotive was heading back south towards Carlisle, news broke of the death of the Earl of Lindsay, owner of 3442. As a mark of respect, the SVR support crew attached a wreath to the locomotive for its next run, a southbound charter on the S&C on 5th August 1989. 3442 is seen south of Cumwhinton.

Driver David Gardner makes a spirited departure from Garsdale as he heads for Carlisle with class V2 No. 4771 *Green Arrow* on 16th September 1989.

On Saturday 24th February 1990, Severn Valley Railway (SVR) based A4 pacific No. 60009 was booked to work a charter train from Carlisle to Leeds and to return with a northbound working the next day. The southbound train was worked as normal until the water-stop at Garsdale from which point matters became so serious that the locomotive was taken off the train at Skipton. The reason why such drastic action had to be taken was due to copious amounts of water seeping into the firebox which was obviously hampering the locomotive's performance with such a heavy train. The A4, which had just returned to traffic from a major overhaul, was retired to the Keighley and Worth Valley Railway, whilst another SVR based locomotive, K4 No. 3442 *The Great Marquess*, which happened to be on Upperby depot, was hastily arranged to cover the following day's return working. Unfortunately, I had to decline a late request to join the K4 support crew due to work commitments later that day. The second day's charter was re-arranged to be steam-hauled from Carlisle instead of the advertised northbound run from Leeds and the K4 is seen heading the train south at Howe & Co signal box, but when the locomotive later returned to Carlisle, it too was found to be suffering from water seeping into the firebox. Suspicion soon fell onto the water that had been taken at Garsdale, a supply which originated from a natural source on the fell side. Heavy rain had fallen in the area for a number of days prior to the running of these charter trains, and it was thought that the water may have contained a higher level of acid than normal. A sample of water was sent for analysis which confirmed that it was unsuitable for steam locomotive boilers.

During 1990, a number of Cumbrian Mountain Express charters involved the use of two steam locomotives with the changeover taking place either at Appleby or Carlisle. Here we see Coronation pacific No. 46229 *Duchess of Hamilton* starting to move the empty stock back into Appleby station in readiness for the southbound working on 25th August 1990. The figure seen on the right, leaning against a post, is John Cameron, owner of A4 60009, which had brought the train north.

Once 46229 had cleared the environs of Appleby station, the A4 was able to propel down towards the signal box to await signals for its move to Upperby. It will be noticed that the locomotive has a somewhat shorter nameplate than its more usual *Union of South Africa* variety. The name *Osprey* was used for a while due to certain political issues at that time.

71000 *Duke of Gloucester* is pictured on the 23rd September 1990 passing Settle Junction, ready to face 15 miles of a near unrelenting gradient of 1 in 100 up to Blea Moor. In order to be fully prepared for such an arduous climb, the fireman will have started to build a thick enough fire and ensuring he had a healthy boiler water level, from some miles distant. Photo: Peter Fitton

After detaching from its train at Citadel station, 71000 has retraced its steps down to London Road Junction from where it can then gain access to the 'through siding' line to travel chimney first on its way to the Upperby depot. In completing this manoeuvre, the locomotive will have negotiated two sides of a triangle which will eventually turn 71000 in readiness for its next working south on the S&C.

On 20th October 1990, the Cumbrian Mountain Express was again shared with two locomotives with the changeover point this time occurring at Carlisle. *Duchess of Hamilton* had charge of the northbound train, and here we see double-chimney Jubilee No. 45596 *Bahamas* approaching Petteril Bridge Junction with the return working. The red line seen running along a number of the coaches is actually a reflection from a red aspect situated at London Road Junction. Support crew members that are leaning out of the leading coach appear to be eagerly anticipating their run on the S&C, but unfortunately within one mile, the locomotive had slipped to a stand in Scotby cutting. It was the second locomotive within days to suffer such a fate.

After 71000 had worked a northbound CME into Carlisle on the 17th November 1990, 6201 *Princess Elizabeth* was given the road with the return working and is seen negotiating the point-work to leave the bi-directional line to approach London Road Junction. Once through the nearby bridge, 6201 will then gain access to the S&C at Petteril Bridge Junction. Of note is the presence of an 'Ethel' train heating unit. These units were converted from redundant Class 25 diesel locomotives and this particular one was the second to be commissioned and was based at Upperby during February 1987 for use on the S&C. They were extremely unpopular with steam charter passengers and lineside photographers alike until they were replaced by a more authentic-looking generator coach in February 1991.

With a diesel-hauled charter train occupying one of the roads beside Appleby signal box, 71000 *Duke of Gloucester* has been called forward to vacate the remaining road to allow 46203 *Princess Margaret Rose* access with the empty stock of the Cumbrian Mountain Express on 1st June 1991. 71000 would then attach to the rear of the stock in order to be in position for the return up working. Crowds have packed Appleby station to see 46203 appear on her first visit to the line.

Footplate Inspector Jim McClelland keeps a watch on proceedings at Appleby on 22nd June 1991 as 6201 *Princess Elizabeth* passes with the empty stock. This was the first time that the two Princess Royal pacifics had been together since their days in store at Kingmoor shed following withdrawal from service during 1962. *Princess Margaret Rose* waits patiently to take over the train to make her first attempt at the southbound climb to Ais Gill. Although I had gained firing experience on preserved lines, this occasion was the beginning of my training to becoming a main-line fireman when Paul Kane handed me the firing shovel to take Maggie up the bank to Garsdale. The only instructions were that the 'flap' had to remain in the up position, which meant that the firebox-door was reduced in size considerably, and that firing had to be constant – one pause and the shovel would be taken from me. What made the temperature rise even more so was the sight of 'speed-king' Willie Alexander sitting in the driver's seat. Personal pride was certainly at stake, but although the 'Blue Riband' was not to be taken that day, I made sure that Paul never saw the shovel again until I handed it back to him at Garsdale.

The water column on the up platform at Appleby station was officially opened on 24th August 1991. Once again, the two Princess Royal pacifics were to share the Cumbrian Mountain Express which was to coincide with the opening ceremony to acknowledge the project jointly undertaken by the Friends of the Settle-Carlisle Line (FoSCL) and Appleby Round Table. As 46203 waits by Appleby signal box, 6201, running some 90 minutes late, crosses with the empty stock movement. Once coupled to the train, *Princess Margaret Rose* drew forward towards the column to perform the official opening which was carried out by Ron Cotton, former Settle & Carlisle Line Project Manager. Prior to departure from Appleby, Paul Kane again handed me the shovel to fire the locomotive up to Garsdale. Training was certainly intense!

The Settle-Carlisle railway is close to the hearts of literally thousands of people. Where else would you see crowd scenes such as this for the opening of a water column!

After the run on the 24th August, *Princess Margaret Rose* was stabled at Carnforth until its next working over the line on the 7th September. Planning ahead, I had intended to park my car at Upperby early on the 6th and travel by rail to Carnforth in order to assist with the preparation of 46203. You can image my surprise when I arrived at Upperby to see long departed A4 No. 60027 *Merlin* standing on one of the pit roads. The locomotive was obviously 60009 *Union of South Africa* which had seemingly suffered another identity crises. My plan to visit Upperby so early in the day certainly paid off, as I was offered a lift direct to Carnforth shed by one of the 'fitness to run' examiners.

Standard class No. 70000 *Britannia* has coupled to the stock of the CME and awaits the signal before drawing the train into Appleby station on 7th September1991 for its first preserved appearance on a southbound S&C working. The northbound leg had been worked by 46203 which is marooned at the other end of the train. The picture shows to good effect why some steam locomotives struggle to move the stock from the lines used for stabling at Appleby where the slight incline is compounded by reverse curves. An animated conversation appears to be taking place between Preston based footplate Inspector Jim Baker and fireman Gordon Hodgson prior to the move.

4472 *Flying Scotsman* has cleared London Road Junction from where it has commenced to run on the bi-directional single line section as it nears Citadel station on 16th May 1992. The photograph clearly illustrates the former up main line that was truncated into a siding which is occasionally employed for stabling charter train stock. There are reports that this line is to be re-instated as a running line which will necessitate the relaying of a mere 100 yards of track in order to bridge the gap between the buffer stop and London Road Junction; it begs the question as to why did they lift it in the first place. The land on the left of picture was previously occupied by the Cowans & Sheldon works; a Carlisle based company that specialised in the manufacture of railway items such as breakdown cranes and turntables until production there ceased in 1987.

After being detached from its train in Citadel station, *Flying Scotsman* has then completed a propelling move back to London Road Junction before running chimney first onto the sharply curved line that gives access towards the Upperby depot. This line, which was once double-track, connects to the West Coast Main Line at Upperby Bridge Junction.

Once at Upperby, 4472 combines with A4 No. 60009 *Union of South Africa* to produce an LNER themed picture. As *Flying Scotsman* backs onto a pit road in order to be prepared for its return journey on the S&C, 60009 stands ready to leave the depot to run to Citadel station from where it was to work an SRPS Carlisle to Kilmarnock charter. The West Coast Main Line can be seen in the far distance.

On the 3rd October 1992, the S&C played host to a special charter train hauled by 46229 *Duchess of Hamilton* to celebrate the 85th birthday of railway artist Terence Cuneo. It would appear that footplate Inspector John McCabe has some concerns as to Mr Cuneo's position in relation to the overhead power lines at Carlisle station. Anyone with knowledge of such power lines will tell you that you don't have to actually touch the cable to cause electrocution - electricity with such high power as 25kv can actually jump some distance. Photo: Gordon Hodgson

Matters have been brought to a halt by the signalman at Howe & Co Sidings box on 6th March 1993, and he is seen informing footplate Inspector John McCabe that due to a snapped wire, he is unable to raise the starter signal and that the driver is authorised to pass that signal at danger but to obey all others. He should then show a yellow flag to the driver – exactly like the one he has hidden behind his back.

In order to increase the number of drivers and firemen in the Carlisle steam link, Standard class 4 tank No. 80080 was hired to British Railways for crew training purposes for a three week period commencing on 22nd February 1993. With the locomotive being provided from my own group, I was on support crew duties for the full period, usually with just one other colleague - Mick Boothby. 80080 was based at the Upperby depot throughout this period, and in addition to the support coach, the train was made up of three coaches borrowed from the 'West Highland' set. The training runs involved two journeys per day between Carlisle and Kirkby Stephen, and were open to pay-on-the-day passengers for a flat fare of £10. With the first of the runs timed to depart Citadel station at 8am, my day normally began some two hours earlier in order to prepare the fire etc, and ended after disposal duties had been completed some 12 hours later. I have no hesitation in stating that this was one of the most exacting periods that I had spent working with steam; actually if truth be known, I was quite relieved to see the locomotive return to Butterley at the end of the 3rd week!

80080 is pictured shortly after taking water at Appleby on the 2nd March 1993 with the ex Carlisle 0800 train.

After having completed a run-round manoeuvre, 80080 draws the coaching stock into the former cattle dock siding at Kirkby Stephen to await the passage of a down service train. It was this ex Leeds service which provided the bulk of the passengers who took the unique opportunity to travel on a genuine S&C steam-hauled stopping train.

This was the scene on the 1st March with near white-out conditions prevailing – snow was actually being blown right through the cab form one side to the other. Reflecting upon the history of the line, it makes one wonder how those Midland Railway crews managed on days like this on locomotives such as the Kirtley 2-4-0 class, the cab of which could best be described as somewhat spartan.

Another view (top) of the early morning train as it stands at a cold Armathwaite station on the 4th March 1993. Throughout the three week programme, I had tried to affix the correct shed-plate to correspond with whoever was driving the locomotive. Seen as two former Kingmoor men, (Paul Kane and John Finlinson), were rostered during this second week, I had fitted original 12A and 68A plates. In a railway city like Carlisle, old rivalries die hard, so care had to be taken that a 'foreign' plate wasn't utilised. Unfortunately, that plan was thrown into disarray later that day when Jimmy Inglis (bottom) appeared for the afternoon run. Jim, a Train Crew Supervisor at Glasgow Central, had been a fireman at Glasgow Corkerhill shed, and had obviously retained his contacts within the Carlisle steam link. It was whilst servicing 80080 at Upperby over the lunch-time break that Jim had taken the opportunity to fit his original 67A (Corkerhill) shed-plate - he even brought his own paraffin lamp! The regulation lamps will be noticed as being in the correct position for a stopping train although its use on the top iron caused some consternation with the Overhead Line Supervisor at Carlisle. The lady seen walking towards the camera and wearing a high-vis coat, is Kath Smith, long time occupant of the FoSCL shop at Appleby station.

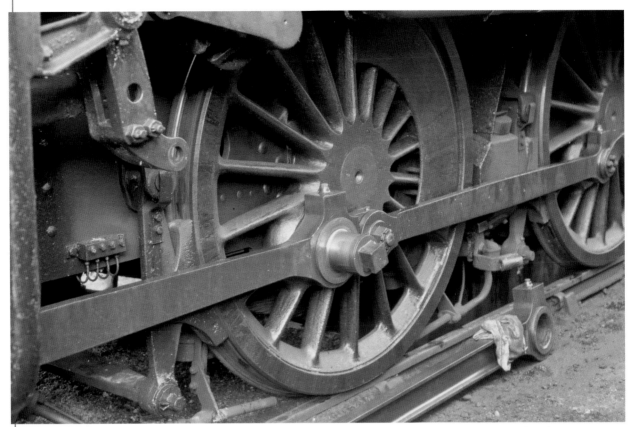

The afternoon return run from Kirkby Stephen on Monday 8th March came to an abrupt halt whilst passing the site of the former Cowans & Sheldon works in Carlisle. A loud banging noise had caused driver Gordon Hodgson (12C shed-plate) to immediately pull up, and a quick examination revealed that a big-end bearing had ran hot. The remainder of the journey into Citadel station, and then onto Upperby, was undertaken at near walking speed. Once at Upperby, in addition to the usual disposal duties, the connecting rod was taken down whilst BR officials were busy putting updates onto local BBC radio stations at Leeds and Carlisle, as trains by the middle of the second week had been standing-room only. Arrangements were hastily arranged for the necessary repair to be undertaken at Carnforth the following day. As that day dawned, I had to source a hire van large enough to hold the connecting rod before loading the offending item (pictured) for the journey to Carnforth. The image (below) shows the newly white-metalled bearing being machined. Upon return to Upperby, the connecting rod was immediately re-fitted and the locomotive prepared for the following day's run.

Friday 12th March 1993 – the final day. This is the lunch-time scene at Upperby with 80080 being coaled prior to the afternoon working to Kirkby Stephen. We have a bigger support crew than usual as a number of our team have travelled up to Carlisle in order to return the locomotive to Butterley at 1830hrs that same day. NRM staff are preparing 46229 *Duchess of Hamilton* for a run over the S&C the following day.

The purpose of the training programme was to allow 5 long-serving firemen to be passed-out as steam locomotive drivers. After each driver had completed four training runs, Chief Traction Inspector Bill Andrew was on the footplate each Friday in order to assess and pass-out the candidates. In addition to demonstrating their locomotive handling skills, drivers were also put through an examination during the layover at Kirkby Stephen on subjects that are close to the hearts of all steam-men; 'the passage of steam', and 'round the wheel'.

Ian Howson undertakes his theory test at Kirkby Stephen on 26th February 1993.

I should add here, that all five drivers qualified, but in addition to their new-found status, they still doubled-up as fireman for some years.

On Friday 14th May 1993, 46203 *Princess Margaret Rose* travelled from its base at Butterley to Keighley to be in position to work a northbound Cumbrian Mountain Express from Lostock Hall the following day. Here we see the locomotive – after a quick cleaning session - stabled on the Keighley & Worth Valley Railway side of the station. The locomotive was always cleaned with an oil and paraffin mix which gave a pleasing finish as shown here. The downside to this method was if it rained, as that would result in the removal of the shiny effect to leave a very dull and flat surface. Another negative to this type of cleaning method was that the oil/paraffin mix acted like a magnet to substances emanating from the chimney – especially prevalent on the S&C whilst running through the numerous tunnels on the line.

The former LMS stronghold at Upperby plays host to two LNER A4 pacifics in May 1993, as a Garter Blue liveried 4498 *Sir Nigel Gresley* stands smokebox to smokebox with BR liveried 60009 *Union of South Africa*. The A4 Locomotive Society appeared to be that more trustworthy than their Scottish counter-parts as the 60009 crew had removed the chime whistle for safe keeping.

Having increased the number of available steam crews at Carlisle during 1993, David Ward issued an instruction that all steam work on the S&C would be handled by that depot and a pool of locomotives was allocated to Upperby for that summer season. This arrangement meant that there was a significant increase in locomotive positional runs to and from Farington (WCML south of Preston), the point where steam exchanged with electric traction. Northbound CME workings over the S&C required the chosen steam locomotive to depart Upperby for the run to Farington shortly after the early-turn signalmen had reported for duty, and with a solitary paper delivery-boy as the only witness to the event, 46203 *Princess Margaret Rose* takes water at Appleby on 24th July 1993 whilst en route to Farington. It was during this year that Halogen headlights began to be seen on steam locomotives, one of which is positioned on 46203's centre lamp-iron.

In order to commemorate the 25th anniversary of BR's final steam hauled train, the infamous 1T57, three locomotives were assembled at Upperby on Tuesday 10th August 1993 to be prepared for the following day's run. Although the original 1T57 (1968) had used the S&C to travel from Liverpool to Carlisle, the 1993 version simply followed the template of a modern-day Cumbrian Mountain Express, running between Leeds and Carlisle. 46229 *Duchess of Hamilton* left Upperby early on the Wednesday to travel to Leeds prior to hauling 1T57 to Carlisle, whilst a double-headed combination of 44871 and 45596 *Bahamas* returned the train over the S&C. Of the three locomotives used, 44871 was the only one to have been involved with 1T57 on that momentous 1968 day.

Former Kingmoor Driver Willie Milne and Inspector Jim McClelland are pictured in the cab of *Princess Margaret Rose* whilst at speed near Dent on the 2nd October 1993 with a Cumbrian Mountain Express from Bradford Foster Square to Carlisle. The locomotive is being driven in typical Carlisle fashion – regulator up in second valve coupled with a short cut-off – a setting that will have been appreciated by the fireman if no-one else. I had fired the locomotive from Bradford up to Blea Moor and I can honestly say that Willie Milne gave me one of the easiest turns I ever had on the S&C; must have been a light load!

Regular visitors to the line will probably recognize all too well the weather conditions seen here from the cab of 46203 as it approaches Blea Moor signal box with a Derby to Carlisle express on the 18th March 1994. The upper reaches of the S&C can be the most inhospitable of places and offers little shelter from the driving rain that is all too prevalent at certain times of the year.

Another event which demonstrates the variety that the preserved steam era has brought to the S&C took place on the 12th February 1994 with a rare appearance to the line of a GWR Castle class locomotive. 5029 *Nunney Castle* shoots a volcano- like smoke effect high into the sky as it runs on the single line section from Ribblehead Viaduct towards Blea Moor box.

After being 'put inside' behind Appleby signal box to allow the passage of a down service train, 5029 propels the empty stock into the station before resuming its journey north. Footplate Inspector Jim McClelland, who is having a passing conversation with fireman Ian Howson, obviously prefers the opportunity for some exercise.

Due to a clearance issue within Citadel station, the steam leg of the charter was terminated south of Carlisle at Howe & Co Sidings from where the return working was diesel hauled. 5029 makes an impressive sight as it undertakes a propelling manoeuvre prior to detaching from the train to travel light engine to Upperby.

Nunney Castle seems to have gained a support coach since its northbound run, and is pictured making a vigorous attempt on the climb near Helm on 12th March 1994 with the southbound charter. Unfortunately, the locomotive came to a stand near Kirkby Stephen and required diesel assistance for the remainder of its journey. As a result of the blockage, lengthy delays were caused to a number of southbound trains including some that had been diverted from the WCML. As one can imagine, BR management were less than impressed and made arrangements for the locomotive to be double-headed on its remaining booked workings. Photo: Gordon Hodgson

On 19th March 1994, 46203 *Princess Margaret Rose* worked a southbound Thames Clyde Express which coincided with the last day at work for Driver David Gardner and Footplate Inspector Jim McClelland. This was a heavy train consisting of 12 coaches in addition to a class 47 diesel locomotive that was attached to the rear; the added weight of the diesel meant that the train was now equal to approximately15 coaches.

The view from Appleby North signal box shows David performing a run-past for the benefit of those assembled on the down platform. I always had mixed feelings concerning the benefits of these events – yes they allowed the fare-paying passenger to see and photograph the locomotive at work, but the downside was that they usually played havoc with the management of the boiler with much lifting of more than one safety valve for some time afterwards.

A view inside the cab taken that same day as David Gardner offers Jim McClelland his final turn in the driving seat of a steam locomotive. Of note is the Automatic Warning System (AWS) which has clearly activated on the approach to the permanent speed restriction (PSR) situated at the Kirkby Thore mine complex. Jim's reaction to the AWS audible warning has caused the 'sunflower dial' to be displayed on the front of the AWS box and that will act as a visual reminder to him that he is proceeding under caution. This 30mph restriction, which was in place for some 36 years, was eventually removed in 2009 after a massive engineering project which involved the laying of giant concrete slabs upon which the track was then laid.

Also of interest is the locomotive's maximum permitted speed as shown on the inside of the cab roof above the driver's seat. At the beginning of 1994, certain classes of steam locomotives had their maximum allowed speed raised from 60mph to 75mph provided that the locomotive was fitted with a calibrated speedometer and AWS. This increase has obviously caused PRCLT's resident artist to suitably amend the notice, but although it now may show 75mph, the S&C line speed will restrict the locomotive on this occasion to 60mph.

Southern S15 class No. 828 is a long way from its Eastleigh home as it makes a rare visit to the S&C on the 7th May 1994. The locomotive, which had run north the previous week, is pictured leaving Garsdale to run high above Dentdale with the return working. Photo: Martin Welch

Footplate Inspector John McCabe occupies the driver's seat as he accelerates A2 class No. 60532 *Blue Peter* to enter the S&C at Petteril Bridge Junction on Sunday 29th May 1994. Steam-hauled charter trains were usually allowed 50 minutes for the 30 mile Carlisle to Appleby section, and although that may appear to be rather generous, one must bear in mind that the trains frequently grossed to nearly 500 tons, and over the initial 7 miles, the climb away from Carlisle is a near constant 1 in 132. A small matter involving a 60mph line speed also has to be taken into account in addition to the PSR previously mentioned at Kirkby Thore.

On Thursday 21st July 1994, No. 70000 *Britannia* ran 'engine and van' from Upperby to Keighley and is pictured approaching Appleby for its booked water stop.

In order to participate in another programme of runs on the S&C, 46203 *Princess Margaret Rose* returned to the line from her base at Butterley by hauling The Waverley from Derby to Carlisle on Thursday 11th August 1994. After passengers had de-trained at Appleby, 46203 is pictured moving the stock clear of the down main line.

A stop for water at Garsdale affords members of the support crew time to shovel some coal forward in the tender. Although the Stanier designed tender was billed as 'self trimming', in reality this was far from the case, unless that is, one was fortunate to have one of the tenders attached to the Princess Coronation class with its magnificent steam operated coal-pusher. Photo: Gordon Hodgson

A unique occasion is captured from the footplate as 46203 *Princess Margaret Rose* and 45596 *Bahamas* pass at Appleby on 20th August 1994. The signalman obviously didn't want the event to occur within the station precincts, as the 'Home' signal is clearly shown as being 'on'.

Bulleid West Country pacific No. 34027 *Taw Valley* makes an impressive sight as it stands on 'C Road' at Carlisle Citadel station awaiting the arrival of the Cumbrian Mountain Express which it will work south over the S&C. Photo: Gordon Hodgson

A repair to 46203 has required the locomotive to be placed inside the carriage shed at Upperby on 1st September 1994. The shed has a busy look about it, but that didn't prevent an announcement made the following day that the depot was to close on 31st March 1995. That date was to coincide with the end of British Railways, obviously it had been decided that such facilities were not required by the privatised railway. Near to the actual closure date, I was at the depot working on 46203, when I was asked to take a wheelbarrow into the locker-room where a number of staff simply opened their lockers and tipped their personal tools into the wheelbarrow. Such was the amount offered; I made three trips to the support coach laden with tools, many of which had seen service at both Kingmoor and Upperby steam sheds. The Upperby staff, many of whom were looking towards redundancy, were well aware that their tools would see good use maintaining PRCLT's steam fleet for years to come.

A panoramic view of Hellifield on Sunday 4th September 1994 shows *Princess Margaret Rose* stabled there. After hauling a southbound charter to Farington the previous day, the locomotive had then set course for the run back to Upperby but only got as far as Settle Junction. The signalman there informed us that due to a service train having derailed at Blea Moor, the S&C was blocked in both directions and that we would be going no further that night. In order for the locomotive to be stabled near to a known water supply, we had no option but to travel back to Hellifield to spend the night and most of the following day there. The joys of working on a support crew.

Rust shown on the down railhead is a good indicator that engineering work is taking place at some point between Kirkby Stephen and Garsdale. With the up road being used for bi-directional movements, 46203 re-starts a southbound charter from Kirkby Stephen after stopping to pick up a pilot-man on the 4th March 1995.

To commemorate the passing of British Railways on 31st March 1995, a steam-hauled charter train ran between Carlisle and Liverpool headed by Standards 75014 and 70000 *Britannia*. The pair are seen being marshalled into position at Upperby, a depot that was to officially close that same day, whilst the bottom image shows the locomotives making good progress as they pass Duncowfold, near Cotehill.

75014 was to later develop a fault but was able to remain on the train through to its destination. A certain driver who took over the controls of *Britannia* at Blackburn later commented to me that as well as pulling the train, he also had to push 75014 all the way to Liverpool!

I have to stress that I had full permission from the signalman at Low House Crossing to capture this shot of 71000 *Duke of Gloucester* as it heads south towards Armathwaite on 29th April 1995.

Princess Royal No. 46203 stands at Hellifield on Tuesday 9th April 1996 with a 520 ton Crewe to Carlisle Cumbrian Mountain Express. As a result of some lively running from Blackburn, we had approached Hellifield some 20 minutes early only to be held at signals outside the station for 19 minutes in order for a Leeds to Carlisle service train to make its booked stop there. Once that train had left Hellifield, the CME was allowed into the station to await the service train to clear the section between Settle Junction and Blea Moor box. This unexpected stop at least allowed the passengers the opportunity to stretch their legs and have a look at the locomotive from close-quarters; but as it turned out, this was to be Maggie's last run before being unexpectedly withdrawn from service.

During the weeks leading up to this charter, a number of small boiler tubes had required some attention, but when the locomotive arrived on Upperby depot, the indication from the chimney meant that matters were not looking at all good and it was obvious that water was leaking into the firebox. Three days later, I was able to climb into a still very warm firebox and this is the sight that greeted me. This is the tubeplate situated in the combustion chamber above the concrete arch. The water staining is quite obvious but notice the tube situated at the 6 o' clock position, from which water is spurting into the firebox. After taking all matters into consideration, a decision was taken to officially withdraw the locomotive from service - slightly earlier than planned.

The recovery of 46203 back to its Butterley base couldn't be arranged until 29th May 1996. The cause of the delay was the time taken to source a sufficient number of vacuum braked vehicles which would provide adequate brake power for the move. The cavalcade is seen passing the former site of the Midland Railway steam shed at Durranhill on the outskirts of Carlisle. Personally, this was a very sad occasion, considering the amount of time I had spent, with others, looking after PMR, a locomotive that had never failed in traffic during the six years spent on the main line. Previously, we (PRCLT) would have returned 46203 to main line duties in the shortest time possible, but two months earlier, Brell Ewart and I had travelled to Bressingham and had returned to Butterley with 6233 *Duchess of Sutherland*. The bad news for Maggie was that work was already in hand to return a Duchess to the main line.

GWR King No. 6024 *King Edward I* certainly added a lot of interest with its appearances on the S&C, but for one reason or another, the steaming capabilities of the King and Castle class locomotives suffered greatly on the heavily graded sections of the line even though 6024 shows no lack of effort as it passes Keld on the 14th March 1998. Photo: Peter Fitton

A blue liveried Southern Merchant Navy class No. 35005 *Canadian Pacific* made a rare appearance to the line on the 29th May 1999. In common with other Southern locomotives to appear on the S&C, the Cumbrian Mountain Express headboard has been suitably customised. Photo: Gordon Hodgson

As a result of the railway industry being privatised, the usual servicing and stabling facilities for steam locomotives visiting Carlisle eventually came under the ownership of EWS. This became a problem for those locomotives working into the city using a different Train Operating Company (TOC), in so much that open access was denied to the Upperby pit-roads. Consequently other sites had to be sourced within the city. Working under the West Coast Railway banner, class B1 No.1264, accompanied by 48151, made a proving run from Hellifield on the 8th June 1999 and the pair are seen after being serviced at London Road yard prior to their return working. With road vehicle access being a pre-requisite to a suitable servicing facility, this location soon became unavailable for such use upon the closure of the adjacent British Fuels depot.

Due to the aforementioned restrictions, steam locomotives were by now being diagrammed to work into the city and then turned to return the charter south later that same day. With an obvious increase in mileage, coal in addition to water had to be loaded into the tender during the layover in Carlisle. Once again a suitable site had to be sourced and when I submitted my tour plan, I included this location on the 'through siding' line at Upperby. This is the line mentioned in previous captions that connects London Road Junction with the WCML at Upperby Bridge Junction. With it being a through line you can probably guess what the initial reaction was from Railtrack, but as the line only saw an average of two freight trains per day, I eventually succeeded in getting the use of it for a twenty minute service stop. Planning this sort of event was similar to planning a military operation. First of all the coal had to be loaded into a number of one ton bags before being transported by road from Butterley to Carlisle for initial storage, then brought to Upperby at the required time for loading by means of a vehicle equipped with a hiab. Here we see one of the bags being manoeuvred into position prior to the support crew member pulling the release rope at the base of the bag. Whilst this is being done, water is being pumped into the tender, the fire will be getting cleaned out, somebody else will have crawled underneath the locomotive to clean the ash-pans, whilst others will be undertaking mechanical examinations/oiling-up duties etc.

Another Hellifield to Carlisle working, this time featuring GWR No. 5972 *Olton Hall*, is seen passing Howe & Co Sidings on a bitterly cold 19th December 1999. This Carnforth based locomotive certainly bucked the trend as far as the performance on the line of GWR engines was concerned; after all, both Castle and King had combined on previous occasions to set the standard for Swindon designed locomotives on the S&C.

In more recent times, Railtrack, then Network Rail, have undertaken a massive programme to improve the condition of the track and various other structures along the line. To mark the completion of one such engineering project, it was decided that the last of the spent ballast held at Ribblehead Quarry would be moved to Carlisle Network Yard by steam. This event took place on Tuesday 19th December 2000 with Stanier class 8F No. 48151 heading, what is believed to be, the heaviest steam-hauled train to be seen on the S&C since BR steam days. The locomotive is pictured getting hold of the 840 ton train as it crosses Ribblehead Viaduct en-route to Carlisle. Photo: Peter Fitton

In order commemorate the 125th anniversary of the opening of the Settle-Carlisle Railway, a steam-hauled charter was organised from Manchester Victoria to Carlisle and return on Tuesday 1st May 2001. Footplate crew members Brian Grierson and Gordon Hodgson pose in front of Black 5 No. 45157 (actually 45407) at Upperby prior to the return journey. Photo: Gordon Hodgson

Coronation class No. 6233 *Duchess of Sutherland* was withdrawn from BR service at Edge Hill shed, Liverpool, during 1964. From then, she was displayed at the Butlins Heads of Ayr holiday camp until 1971, when on the 1st March that year, 6233 was moved again, by rail, to her new home at the Bressingham steam museum in Norfolk. The route used to move the locomotive from Ayr to Norwich included the Settle-Carlisle line. Thirty-one years after that event, *Duchess of Sutherland* returned to the S&C, this time in steam, heading a Crewe to Carlisle charter on 29th June 2002. What is even more remarkable is that the event took place eighteen days after the locomotive had hauled the Royal Train, conveying Her Majesty the Queen, on part of her Golden Jubilee Year tour – the first time a steam locomotive had been entrusted with that task in 35 years.

A view from the fireman's seat as 6233 crosses Ribblehead Viaduct which clearly illustrates the work carried out in 1989 that resulted in the track being singled and a 30mph speed restriction being imposed - steam locomotives are further restricted to only 20mph.

(Left) The Settle-Carlisle Railway seen at its best as 6233 *Duchess of Sutherland* approaches Lunds Viaduct whilst heading a Carlisle to Derby express on 20th July 2002. The black smoke is an indication that the locomotive has just received a round of firing which signifies that we are not due to stop at Garsdale which is only one mile distant. By this time, the Garsdale water-stop was being omitted by many groups, primarily as a result of a number of locomotives having had their tender water capacities increased enabling them to complete the section between Appleby and Hellifield with ease. Another issue was that the under-track pipe-work at Garsdale required replacing, and with MSLOA (formerly SLOA) not keen to fund the cost of the repairs, the watering facility was eventually withdrawn from use in July 2003.

As usual with today's steam fleet, the locomotive is well turned-out. Unlike 46203, *Duchess of Sutherland*'s paintwork was maintained with a high grade polish. Usually, two coats of polish would be applied whilst the locomotive was at its home depot, and this was maintained whilst away from base with an energy-saving wash/wax solution. At least if it rained, the locomotive still looked in pristine condition which was undoubtedly an improvement on the oil/paraffin mix type of cleaning.

(Above) It was noticed in a journal issued by The Friends of the Settle-Carlisle Line (FoSCL), that they were keen to mark the 25th anniversary of the death of Bishop Eric Treacy at Appleby station, and they were basically open to ideas how this could be best achieved. I made contact with FoSCL with a suggestion that I could arrange a charter train using 6233 *Duchess of Sutherland* to haul 'The Lord Bishop', if they would be prepared to arrange suitable events at Appleby station. An agreement was soon reached and I subsequently submitted a tour plan to run the charter from Crewe to Carlisle via Shap, and to use the 'through siding' (TS) line at Upperby to gain direct access to the S&C at Petteril Bridge Junction. The TS line hadn't been used by a passenger charter train of any description for I don't know how long. Railtrack's initial response was to refuse the application as the TS was declared as freight only. A friendly reminder was given to Railtrack that due to recent engineering work between London Road Junction and Citadel station, all timetabled passenger traffic from the S&C and Newcastle routes had used the line to gain access to Citadel station, and therefore their stance could be reasonably challenged. After a short period of reflection, permission was then granted to use the line and the train ran as intended to give passengers on the sell-out train a day to remember with the prospect of Grayrigg, Shap, Ais Gill and Wilpshire climbs. Those negotiations to secure the use of the TS line have since led to the wider use of that facility by a number of other tour promoters. After the proceedings at Appleby had been completed, 6233 *Duchess of Sutherland* is back in action crossing Arten Gill Viaduct on 17th May 2003 displaying an original headboard from one of the 1978 Lord Bishop trains. Photo: John Stiles

(Right) In addition to remembering Eric Treacy, one of the main events held at Appleby that day, was the presentation of one of the Bishop Eric Treacy nameplates from a recently withdrawn class 86 electric locomotive, to the Friends of the Settle-Carlisle Line for display at Appleby station. The nameplate was received on behalf of the FoSCL by the Bishop of Carlisle, the Right Reverend Graham Dow. The Bishop, who happens to be a steam enthusiast and Vice President of FoSCL, kindly posed for this photograph before our departure from Appleby.

Shortly after I had resigned from my positions with the PRCLT in 2004, 6233 was allocated a second Royal Train working, this time conveying HRH the Prince of Wales from Settle to Carlisle on the 22nd March 2005. In addition to officially opening the newly re-furbished station building at Kirkby Stephen, the Prince also took time to visit Appleby station.

6233 is seen approaching Horton in Ribblesdale displaying a rather attractive headboard depicting the Prince of Wales' official coat of arms rather than the three feathered variety which I think most people would have expected. The headboard had been made by Andrew Wagstaff, a member of the PRCLT team.

71000 *Duke of Gloucester* climbs through Scotby cutting with the Dalesman on the 3rd September 2005. With the cutting being heavily tree-lined, it is understandable how this area became a problem during the leaf fall season which resulted in more than one steam-hauled train slipping to a stand. Modern methods employed to clean the rail-head appear to have negated this problem.

A wintry scene at Ribblehead on the 29th December 2005 has created a near silhouette image of Black 5 No. 45407 leading Standard class 4 No. 76079 across the viaduct as they forge north towards Blea Moor. A snow covered Ingleborough adds to the chill factor which will have no doubt been thoroughly appreciated by the photographer. Photo: Peter Fitton

High summer at Ais Gill Viaduct as 6233 *Duchess of Sutherland* climbs towards the summit on 1st July 2006 with just a haze at the chimney top. Purists would point out that that is exactly how it should be.

With my part-time railway career at an end, events have moved in a full circle and I am now back on the other side of the fence, so to speak. Once again, another Wagstaff headboard adorns the locomotive. One of the structures that feature in many photographs taken from this location is Hangman's Bridge which is seen towards the rear of the train. Unfortunately, this iconic wooden-structured occupation bridge was demolished during one of the engineering blockades on the line during 2009.

Southern King Arthur class No. 30777 *Sir Lamiel* runs out of the shade and into more favourable light as it passes Low House Crossing, near Armathwaite, with the up 'Dalesman' on 27th August 2006. After being recently painted, the signal box has had an additional name-board fitted which has been placed above the box windows rather than the customary lower position once favoured by the Midland Railway Co.

Standing-in for 4771 *Green Arrow* on a York to Carlisle charter, *Sir Lamiel* speeds towards Armathwaite on 17th September 2006. Photographic pan shots can be difficult to execute, but very rewarding if they come out right.

Coronation 6233 *Duchess of Sutherland* leaves a smoke trail in the Lower Eden Valley as it approaches Armathwaite tunnel on the 8th September 2007 with the Hadrian rail-tour, which involved a rather circuitous route from York-Gateshead-Carlisle-Leeds and back to York. The headboard had been modelled on a Royal Scot 1951 version.

Scotby village lies within 2 miles of Carlisle and once had the distinction of having two stations, one provided by the North East Railway and the other by the Midland Railway. The former Midland station was one of the early casualties on the S&C, succumbing to closure in 1942 before being converted into a private dwelling, which is shown here on the 24th May 2008, as Stanier class 8 No. 48151 passes with a northbound charter. The NER station closed during 1959.

Bulleid Pacific No. 34067 *Tangmere* made a rare appearance on the line on the 31st May 2008 whilst substituting at short notice for Stanier 8F 48151. With smoke still visible near to the northern portal of Armathwaite Tunnel, 34067 will soon pass Low House Crossing signal box to commence the final descent towards Carlisle.

On the same day that *Tangmere* ran north on the S&C, 6201 *Princess Elizabeth* was also at work on the line at the head of a Pathfinder Railtour which is pictured storming towards the summit at Ais Gill.

With steam locomotives now predominantly working 'out and back' on the S&C, southbound departures from Carlisle can be some three to four hours later than they were in earlier years, a situation that can occasionally coincide with the train running through stunning evening light. This is demonstrated here with another appearance of 6201 which is seen at Birkett whilst en-route to Liverpool on Saturday 2nd August 2008. One downside to more recent steam-hauled charter workings though, has been the occasional use of multi-liveried coaching stock – illustrated here with no fewer than four different liveries on display.

After an absence of 10 years, A4 Pacific No. 60007 *Sir Nigel Gresley* returned to the S&C with a Hellifield to Carlisle train on the 1st November 2008. The locomotive is painted in an attractive BR blue livery - which it actually carried in the early 1950s – and is seen at London Road Junction on its way to Upperby Yard for servicing prior to returning south via the WCML.

Chapter Five – **Monochrome Reprise**

During the formative years of steam operations on the S&C, a number of charter trains featured two locomotives, one of which was employed between Hellifield and Carnforth via the Little North-Western line. On 31st October 1981, 46229 *Duchess of Hamilton* headed a Cumbrian Mountain Pullman from Carlisle and upon arrival at Hellifield, Stanier class 5 No. 5407 has attached to what was the rear of the train in order to take the CMP on its final steam leg across to Carnforth. Light is obviously fading, as the photographer has carried out a time exposure in order to capture the scene. Photo: Martin Welch

As a result of purchasing the eight car Pullman set in 1981, SLOA wasted little time in promoting their charter trains on the S&C under the banner of the 'Cumbrian Mountain Pullman'. Stanier class 5X No. 5690 *Leander* is seen making a spirited departure from Carlisle on the 23rd January 1982 as it heads a CMP to pass the site of the former Durranhill steam shed. This was *Leander's* first visit to the line since the infamous 1980 Garsdale rescue, the intervening period having been spent at the Severn Valley Railway workshops at Bridgnorth where the locomotive had undergone a 'seven-yearly' major overhaul.

As already detailed in Chapter Four, Southern Class N15 No. 777 *Sir Lamiel* made her first visits to the line in the spring of 1982 double-heading two CMP trains with Stanier 5 No. 5407 tucked inside as suitable cover. For *Sir Lamiel*, these were more or less proving runs geared towards further work on the line, and as the pair pass Durranhill on the 3rd April 1982 to begin the initial 1 in 132 climb, it is evident that although both locomotives are not short of steam, 777 is already doing most of the work.

There have been a number of preserved steam locomotives that have made just a solitary visit to the line since 1978, one of those being the Midland Compound No. 1000

Coupled with 5690 *Leander*, No. 1000 had made it's northbound run on the S&C on 5th February 1983, and returned south the following Saturday. The locomotive, under the care of staff from the NRM, is seen being prepared for duty at Carlisle Upperby on Friday 11th February 1983.

The K1 class was introduced in 1949 and was a Peppercorn development of Thompson's K1/1 (61997) and out of a total of 70 locomotives built, 40 of them were based in the north-east. It was therefore appropriate that No. 62005 eventually came into the ownership of the North-East Locomotive Preservation Group (NELPG), who returned it to mainline duty in an LNER guise as No. 2005. The locomotive is pictured at Carlisle on 20th March 1983 after detaching from the SLOA Pullman set.

For a period during the early 1980s, a number of steam workings on the S&C were coupled with Cumbrian Coast line duty running between Carnforth and Sellafield. After hauling a Cumbrian Coast Express from Carnforth, the locomotive would then travel light engine from Sellafield to Upperby to be in position to work a southbound S&C charter the following day. The same working practice was occasionally employed in the opposite direction. 4472 *Flying Scotsman* is pictured at Upperby on Friday 17th June 1983 being prepared for the following day's Cumbrian Coast Express.

Flying Scotsman is back in action on the S&C at Langwathby with a mid-week up Cumbrian Mountain Pullman on 29th June 1983. Dick Hardy, a former LNER man, occupies the fireman's seat and appears to be checking the condition of the smoke at the chimney top. When I later put it to him that the black exhaust was somewhat uncharacteristic for an A3, he was quick to point out that the fireman had actually been an LMS man!

Stanier Black Five 5407 passes the summit board at Ais Gill on the 24th August 1983 with what is believed to be the final appearance on the line of SLOA's Pullman set prior to them being withdrawn from service to allow the removal of asbestos, traces of which, had been discovered in the vehicles.

Former firing instructors may wish to avert their eyes from the sight of 46229 *Duchess of Hamilton* blackening the sky over Appleby on 4th February 1984. Although photographers have always appreciated a bit of black smoke, it would appear that the fireman has over-cooked it somewhat as 46229 comes to a stand opposite the box after completing a run-past through the station.

By contrast, a haze at an LNER chimney, as A4 No. 60009 *Union of South Africa* passes over Culgaith level crossing with a southbound Cumbrian Mountain Express on 24th April 1984. Alas, if all of you Doncaster fans are feeling a bit smug comparing this with 46229's volcano, all is not what it seems. The A4, which had taken over the train at Howe & Co signal box, promptly began to set fire to half of Cumbria.

Long Meg sidings will always be remembered as the starting point of those 8F and 9F hauled anhydrite trains that were such a feature on the line in the 1960s. This view, taken on 9th August 1984, shows the track and signalling still intact as 46229 *Duchess of Hamilton* passes with an up charter. By this time, the sidings hadn't seen any use for some years, and the 1955 built signal box was permanently 'switched out' as a result of its closure during 1983.

The oldest box still operating on the S&C can be found at Low House Crossing, about a mile north of Armathwaite. Constructed during 1890, the box controls one of the two level crossings situated on the line, the other one, which we have already seen, is located at Culgaith which happens to be the next box to the south. Southern Light Pacific, No 34092 *City of Wells* approaches the boarded level crossing on 23rd August 1984 to begin the long descent towards Carlisle.

After being stabled for four days at Upperby, *City of Wells* returned south with a Cumbrian Mountain Express. The photograph was taken from Low House Crossing signal box as the locomotive was recovering from an adverse distant signal. It was only when 34092 began to appear slowly coming into view around the curve that the home signal was lifted which resulted in an immediate reaction from the driver which produced this rather impressive smoke effect.

A night-time study of a Duchess, as 46229 simmers gently at Upperby on Friday 7th December 1984 prior to the following day's encounter with the S&C.

Another night shot, this time at Citadel station on 28th March 1985 with 5690 *Leander* coupled ahead of 44767 **George Stephenson**, as the locomotives await signals on their way to Millerhill and Perth respectively. The pair had double-headed a fourteen coach train, originally rostered to 46229, from Manchester to Carlisle via the S&C some days previous.

On the 20th April 1985, Class 5X No. 5690 *Leander* retraced part of the route of the Thames Clyde Express from Kilmarnock to Hellifield. Some days previous, I was approached by Carlisle photographer Bob Leslie who enquired if there was any chance of some black smoke being provided for his benefit at Drybeck Viaduct, near Armathwaite. As you can see his request was duly acted upon - with the added bonus of fireman Gordon Hodgson and myself getting in on the act! Photo: Robert Leslie

Another look at *Kolhapur*'s visit to the line on the 21st March 1987, this time recorded from Kirkby Stephen signal box, as the locomotive heads north with a Cumbrian Mountain Express. A snow covered Wild Boar fell can just be seen in the far distance.

Kolhapur's return working occurred four weeks later on 18th April 1987 whilst in charge of the Mancunian, which is seen south of Cumwhinton. Unfortunately, the celebrated return to the line was marred with the locomotive running a 'hot box' later that day at Derby whilst it was returning to its home base at Tyseley.

The Stanier 4000 gallon tender has been acquired since the last time I had photographed 45593 at Carlisle in 1966 when it was then paired with the smaller Stanier 3500 gallon version.

The regulator has been eased to allow *Mallard* to coast down to Petteril Bridge Junction from where it will gain access to the S&C for its final visit to the line on 27th August 1988. For S&C bound trains, this junction has a 20mph speed restriction, and an 'approach control' signal is situated there to regulate the speed of the approaching train. Although the road will have been set, the signal will continue to show a red aspect until the passage of the slowly advancing locomotive automatically triggers a change of signal, provided that the section ahead is clear. Obviously, if that section is already occupied, the train will be brought to a stand at the signal.

Southern Merchant Navy No. 35028 *Clan Line* makes an impressive sight as it passes through Armathwaite on 8th April 1989 with an up Cumbrian Mountain Express. The specially manufactured headboard, and the white coloured discs being used instead of the more common paraffin lamps, help to give a real Southern flavour to the event. The 1899 built signal box, which was de-commissioned on the 15th January 1983, has since been preserved in situ and restored into original Midland Railway colours.

After receiving a heavy round of firing, LNER V2 No. 4771 *Green Arrow* exits Scotby cutting to pass milepost number 305 on 30th September 1989. The over-bridge seen to the rear of the train is situated some ten minute walking time from my house; fortunate, I know.

A4 No. 60009 is in the process of coupling-up to its support coach prior to leaving Upperby on Saturday 24th February 1990 to work the Carlisle to Leeds charter previously described in Chapter 4, which resulted in the locomotive being removed from the train at Skipton. The Gresley pacific had recently re-entered traffic after a major overhaul at the Severn Valley Railway and was still to be fitted with its *Osprey* nameplates, which it displayed for a period of 18 months, before reverting to *Union of South Africa*.

Another locomotive to return to traffic that year after a major overhaul was 46229 *Duchess of Hamilton* which is seen heading south crossing High Stand Gill Viaduct near Cotehill on 13th April 1990 (Good Friday). This was the locomotive's first run after re-entering traffic and the special train was organised for the benefit of the Friends of the National Railway Museum, from York to Carlisle and return.

The S&C has been used on numerous occasions as a means for moving locomotives up to Fort William for the summer season. Butterley based Black Five No. 44932, not a regular performer on the former Midland line, travelled north to Carlisle on Friday 7th June 1991, and stabled at Upperby for most of that week-end. After propelling its support coach from Upperby to London Road Junction, 44932 is seen resuming its journey to Fort William on the Sunday afternoon.

Those summer stints on the West Highland line were very demanding on support crews, working one week about with the other locomotive based there, and assistance was usually sought from other groups to help share the load. With 44932 being a Butterley based engine, I had no hesitation in going to Fort William to spend a week working on the Black Five during the first week in August; all good experience.

This line-up had been arranged in a local drinking establishment (some days earlier I hasten to add), as 46203 *Princess Margaret Rose* and 6201 *Princess Elizabeth* occupy the tracks at Appleby on 22nd June 1991. 6201, under the command of Driver Ken Stubbs, had arrived with the down Cumbrian Mountain Express, whilst 46203 had ran from Upperby to take the charter back south. Inspector Jim McClelland, seen in conversation with Driver Willie Alexander, had allowed me a few seconds to climb down from the footplate in order to obtain this shot, before 46203 cleared the up main line. Two Princess Royals on the same CME – no wonder the platforms and over-bridge are packed.

Another engine and coach movement from Upperby to Appleby sees 34027 *Taw Valley* diverting on to the S&C at Petteril Bridge Junction on 27th December 1991. I have to confess that the smoke was by prior arrangement.

The only occasion that I ever saw a steam locomotive occupy the loop at Howe & Co Sidings was on 26th September 1992, when A3 pacific No. 4472 *Flying Scotsman* waited upon the arrival of a diesel hauled charter. Matters regarding the locomotive's support crew appeared to be an issue; I say that as a result of receiving a request a few days earlier, asking if I would complete disposal duties whilst the engine was stabled at Upperby. Even though I had no connection with 4472, I undertook those duties, in addition to one or two other matters, but I politely declined the offer to join the seriously depleted support crew. You will notice the lack of a support coach, quite exceptional at this time of steam's presence on the main-line, but it appears that Driver Tommy Hayton has more serious matters on his mind as he heads towards the signalman's kettle.

With up to 5 steam locomotives being based at Upperby during the 1993 summer season, space at the depot was at a premium considering that each locomotive also had a support coach. To overcome this overcrowding, a number of engines, together with their coaches, were stabled at High Wapping sidings which are situated outside the Power Box near to Citadel station. A shunt between the two sites occurred on most Fridays, but I have to admit pulling a few local strings to ensure that 46203 was at Upperby more than it was at High Wapping. Normally, after a run up to Carlisle on a Saturday, I would undertake disposal duties on the Wednesday or Thursday, work permitting. This would entail cleaning out the firebox, ash-pans and smokebox before restocking the tender with water and coal. Doing it this way, 46203 was then ready for action at very short notice - especially if the locomotive booked to do the next run became unavailable for one reason or another; an event that actually occurred on more than one occasion. Building up to a run on a Saturday, preparations would begin at Thursday lunch-time from when I would remain with the engine until the run was completed on the Saturday evening.

This is the scene at Upperby on Wednesday 23rd June 1993 with 60532 having been moved from High Wapping on the previous Friday in order for it to be prepared for a six-monthly steam exam. 46203 stands fully prepared before being lit-up the following day; I've obviously even had the time to clean the locomotive.

Ivatt class 2 No. 46441 made a surprise visit to the line on 24th September 1994 working the 'Westmorlander' from Carnforth to Appleby and return. The six coach train is seen entering Settle station. The return from Appleby obviously involved tender-first running, at the same time that 46203 *Princess Margaret Rose* was heading north with a Bradford Foster Square to Carlisle charter. The pair passed each other near to Smardale Viaduct during a heavy downpour of rain. Photo: Martin Welch

October 1st 1994 - another day on the S&C - more rain. Prior to leaving Appleby with *Princess Margaret Rose*, the rostered fireman, John Finlinson, asked if I would fire the locomotive up the bank to Garsdale. I was obviously fully aware that we were due to pass *Duchess of Hamilton* en route to the summit and I was keen to obtain a photograph of the two Stanier pacifics passing each other. I accepted his offer, but first of all I prepared my camera for the impending shot. To my surprise, as soon as we left Appleby, John sat in the fireman's seat and began to open his packed lunch!

As we approached Kirkby Stephen, he noticed that the signals were 'off' for 46229.

The shovel was quickly thrown into the tender as John vacated his seat to allow me to obtain this historic shot as the locomotives met just south of the former goods shed. He then regained his original position, for him to complete his lunch, and me, his firing turn. Shortly after leaving Birkett Tunnel, 46203 began to slip and this continued all the way up to the summit. Speed had dropped alarmingly as former Kingmoor driver, Brian Hayton, fought to keep the 470 ton train moving on a very poor rail. Even though the locomotive was constantly losing her feet, he left the regulator up in the cab roof as he controlled each bout of slipping with continual use of the reverser. There were times when I thought that we would come to a stand but somehow Brian kept the locomotive inching closer to the summit which was approached at a very modest 17mph. Here was a man who was certainly showing us what years of experience can produce when the chips are really down.

When we eventually arrived at the Garsdale water-stop, I congratulated Brian on what had probably been the finest piece of driving that I had the privilege to witness. Obviously referring to the spate of retirements that were to occur, he simply replied, 'Where will you get experience like that when we've all gone'. I later found out that 46229 had also slipped all the way up to the summit on her return working later that same day, but like 46203, she got there. If proof were needed that David Ward was right to place restrictions on steam locomotives using the S&C during the month of October - that was it.

Run-pasts at Appleby are now a thing of the past, which is unfortunate, at least for the paying passenger who appreciated such events. Having completed a run-past on the 30th March 1996, Bill Andrew has time for a passing word with Bernard Staite as he propels the train towards the signal box from where run number two will commence. The distinct lack of people standing on the up platform and on the footbridge was no doubt an early Health & Safety requisite.

A wintry scene at Ais Gill sees Stanier Mogul No. 2968 making its solitary southbound visit to the S&C on 4th January 1997. This unique Severn Valley Railway based locomotive is paired with what appears to be a tender from a Black Five rather than its own 3,500 gallon version.

An all LMS pairing consisting of 48773 and 45407 certainly has a 1960s look about it as they head south towards Birkett Tunnel on 3rd May 1999. The pair had worked north some nine days earlier, and for the 8F, these runs were the only appearances that it has made on the S&C as a preserved locomotive. Formally allocated to Carlisle Kingmoor, it no doubt had previously been a regular on the line during its BR days.

After the dismal performance of a GWR Castle class locomotive on the S&C some seven years earlier, supporters of 'all things Swindon' were obviously keen to set the record straight with another appearance on the line of 6024 *King Edward I* on 10th February 2001. Unfortunately, once again the achilles heel for GWR locomotives (5972 excepted) appears to be the Kirkby Stephen area, for just as *Nunney Castle* expired there, so did the mighty King. As 6024 passes Waitby on its approach to Kirkby Stephen, driver Gordon Hodgson seeks shelter from the relentless driving rain

Chapter Six – The Blue Riband

by Mike Notley

Prior to the advent of 'Open Access', main line steam's confined range and restricted speed served to limit the opportunities for locomotives to be pressed towards the upper ranges of their abilities. Of the regular steam routes, the North Wales Coast was relatively flat and offered little challenge, even with very heavy trains. The Welsh Marches could boast excellent scenery and the climb to Llanvihangel in both directions and the route from Banbury north had Saunderton Bank on which some outstanding performances had been achieved, particularly by 46229. But the route that caught the imagination with its steep gradients, its dramatic setting and occasionally very unfriendly weather was the Settle and Carlisle Line. From its origin the route had provided a searching challenge of both men and machine and names like Ais Gill, Ribblehead and the Long Drag had become a part of railway folklore. Its fame had spread well beyond the enthusiast fraternity and the steam

How it all started. When 46229 *Duchess of Hamilton* worked a northbound charter on 28th May 1983, it was sporting a blue Riband together with a medallion which made reference to the locomotive's performance on its previous southbound working over the S&C. The adornment was a light-hearted taunt from members of the locomotive's support crew, but certain Carlisle based footplate crews where quick to take up the Blue Riband challenge. Photo: Gordon Hodgson

hauled trains that still traversed this spectacular route were popular with the ordinary public who had simply come along to see this famous railway. This meant large trains of up to 14 vehicles, often grossing well over 500 tons, providing challenge enough, but then, in the early 80's, there began an unofficial contest that would catch the imagination of locomotive crews and owning groups alike and result in some of the finest sustained locomotive performances ever recorded. The 'Blue Riband' was born. There are a number of versions of how the contest came into being but it seems most likely to have originated in the ranks of the Carlisle drivers who regularly worked the route. At that time Carlisle could boast a link of outstanding drivers who revelled in the best traditions of great enginemanship and were only too keen to show what they could do. Names like Willie Alexander, Willie Milne, Davy Gardner, Jackie Eden, Kenny Stubbs and the Hayton brothers, Tommy and Brian. And, importantly, they were backed up by some enthusiastic, skilful firemen, many of whom, like Brian Grierson, Gordon Hodgson and Paul Kane are now active steam drivers themselves. And they had the perfect tool in *Duchess of Hamilton* which was a regular sight on the route and, it seems, her NRM minders, at the very least, did not disapprove. The contest was a trial of sustained strength, the 60mph upper limit to which steam was subject at that time preventing all but the most minor of speeding excesses. And the arena for this contest was the 15¼ mile climb from just south of Ormside Viaduct to Ais Gill Summit at Milepost 259¾, the 'Long Drag'. Before continuing to talk about the contest itself, it will help to look in more detail at what faced the contestants.

The challenge

Almost all southbound steam charters over the S & C in the early 80's would have stopped for water at the dairy to the east of the railway just south of Appleby station. This would change with the installation of the water tower in the Up direction at Appleby station in 1991. Leaving the dairy, trains would have less than 2 miles in which to gain impetus before they crossed Ormside Viaduct and began the climb. They were helped in their search for speed by a little over a mile down at 1-in-176 and would be looking to be travelling at close to a mile a minute as they sped high above the Eden and set sail for Ais Gill. The first part of the climb is 3½ miles of 1-in-100 that takes the train through Helm Tunnel to Griseburn Viaduct which carries the line across Helm Beck and marks an easing to 1-in-166. Around Milepost 269½ the gradient eases further, to 1-in-200, to the site of Crosby Garrett station. The next three-quarters of a mile includes two brief level sections

With the Blue Riband still being displayed on the locomotive, Driver Alf Tickner backs 46229 onto the support vehicles at Citadel station on the 30th May 1983 prior to working a southbound CMP, with which he promptly set a new record time of 19 minutes, 25 seconds.

either side of a short 1-in-220, but by the time trains cross Smardale Viaduct, the climb has resumed at 1-in-100. 2½ miles at this gradient carries the line to Kirkby Stephen station after which a brief easing to 1-in-264 provides welcome, if short relief before the 1-in-100 resumes. Birkett Tunnel is notoriously wet and care has to be taken to avoid a slip as you enter, the regulator often being eased slightly at this point in anticipation. Emerging from the tunnel into a damp cutting, the line reaches Milepost 264, usually the slowest point on the whole climb and the beginning of an easing to 1-in-330 for almost a mile as the line makes its way along Mallerstang Common. This gives the locomotive and crew a chance to gather themselves for a final effort as the 1-in-100 resumes around Milepost 263 as the imposing bulk of Wild Boar Fell dwarfs the railway to the right. Curving first right and then left, the line passes under the wooden Hangman's Bridge and over Ais Gill Viaduct, The climb ends at Milepost 260, just before the line passes beneath the B6259, and the track is level as it passes Milepost 259¾ and the painted signs telling that this is Ais Gill Summit, 1,169 feet above sea level. Since passing Milepost 275 the line has climbed a little over 670 feet at an average gradient of 1-in-120. This then was the arena for this contest, but why the 'Blue Riband'? Well, this was the name of an award initiated for publicity purposes by shipping companies in the 1860's and given to the ship recording the fastest transatlantic crossing. To signify its achievement, the ship flew a blue pennant from the topmast, a blue riband. Later the term was to be associated with record achievements of many kinds, particularly in sport.

The contest begins

Its link with the climb of the 'Long Drag' appears to have been initiated in early 1983 when the front of *Duchess of Hamilton* was adorned with a blue ribbon prior to working the 'Cumbrian Mountain Pullman' on 30th May. This was presumably as a result of the same locomotives achievements on 19th April 1983 when, in the hands of Driver Hine, she had worked what was widely acclaimed as the best run since restoration of main line steam operations, setting a time of 19 minutes 31 seconds with a 14-coach 560 ton load over what was to become the 'Blue Riband' stretch. A month later, on 23rd April, she was significantly ahead of this run before being checked to walking pace at Kirkby Stephen. The ribbon seemed to do the trick on 30th May when, driven by Driver Tickner, she clipped 6 seconds off her 19th April time and the contest was born. But every contest has to have rules and it wasn't long before the requirements for satisfying 'Blue Riband' status were 'unofficially' laid down. The title was to go to the locomotive recording the fastest time in preservation between Mileposts 275 and 259¾ hauling a minimum load of 12 coaches. As the Top Six table shows, the weight of 12 coaches could vary considerably depending on the mix of B5/Commonwealth bogied vehicles and the number of passengers. There were also those who suggested that having two people firing should disqualify any run, but, rather than over-complicate things, the simple basic rules stood. With no obvious challenger to her dominance, 46229 had the field to herself for a while and moved the record significantly forward on 7th January

115

A group of retired Carlisle railwaymen, which include a number of Blue Riband activists, pose with a selection of headboards that were once a common sight in the Border city: (L to R) Brian Hayton, Tommy Hayton, Harold Stubbs (former Upperby driver but not on preserved steam), John Duncan (SLOA, CME), Jim McClelland, David Gardner and Ken Stubbs.

1984 when, in the hands of Willie Alexander, she raced up the climb in 17 minutes 56 seconds. She had begun her run from the Appleby dairy and only passed Milepost 275 at 50mph. Remarkably, hauling a load of 13 coaches weighing 485 tons gross, she went on to average 53.5mph for the climb and passed the summit at 53. And there the record rested for a while. *Duchess of Hamilton* was withdrawn from service in October 1985 and, quite honestly, there wasn't anything else on the main line that could get anywhere near her figure. We had to wait 6 years before the record books would be rewritten.

The 'Riband' changes hands

46229 had returned to the main line in 1989 and was followed by *Duke of Gloucester* a year later. On 20th July 1991, the pennant passed to the first locomotive other than the Duchess to hold it since the inception of the idea. That locomotive was 71000 which smashed the Duchess's time by almost a minute, recording 17 minutes exactly and leaving no doubt that this was now not just a contest between footplate crews but also between locomotives. And in early 1992 the return of *Blue Peter* added

THE 'BLUE RIBAND' RECORD			
THE CUMBRIAN MOUNTAIN EXPRESS			
SATURDAY 14th AUGUST 1993			
Locomotive		46229	
Vehicles		12	
Tons tare/ gross		438/460	
Driver		Brian Grierson	
Firemen		Paul Kane/ K P Lees	
Traction Inspector		Jimmy McClelland	
Dist.		Booked	Actual	Speed
m.c.	Timing Point	m.secs	m.secs	mph
0.00	**APPLEBY**	0.00	0.00	-
1.20	Milepost 276		3.25	47
2.20	Milepost 275		4.28	60
3.20	Milepost 274		5.29	58
3.61	Helm Tunnel (in)		6.01	55
4.20	Milepost 273		6.34	55
5.28	Griseburn		7.46	53½
6.20	Milepost 271		8.44	56
7.40	Crosby Garrett		10.00	60
8.20	Milepost 269		10.43	66
9.20	Milepost 268		11.39	62
10.20	Milepost 267		12.40	57
10.53	Kirkby Stephen	14.00	13.06	56½
11.20	Milepost 266		13.43	57
12.20	Milepost 265		14.48	54½
12.58	Birkett Tunnel (in)		15.20	52½
13.20	Milepost 264		15.57	49½
14.00	Mallerstang		16.49	54/55
15.20	Milepost 262		18.10	54½
16.20	Milepost 261		19.17	53
17.20	Milepost 260		20.25	52
17.40	Ais Gill Summit (MP 259¾)	21.00	20.42	54/62
20.47	**GARSDALE**	26.00	24.46	-

a third contender to the mix. On the 21st March 1992, the A2, again in the hands of the irrepressible Willie Alexander and fired by Paul Kane and Gordon Hodgson, recorded a time of 17 minutes 33 seconds, evidence that she too was a serious contender for the crown. But the 60532 challenge never materialised and that time still remains her best effort. The field was down to two. *Duchess of Hamilton* had a 'sighter' on 24th April 1993 when, in the hands of Driver Jackie Eden, she posted a time of 17 minutes 23 seconds, at that stage, second only to the Duke's record but, before the year was out, she would do significantly better.

The record

The weather on 14th August 1993 was cool, dry and calm as the southbound 'Cumbrian Mountain Express' left Appleby on time. The load was 12 coaches of around 470 tons gross and the driver was Brian Grierson. Brian was one of the Carlisle men passed out for driving a couple of years earlier on 80080 and his firemen were Paul Kane and K P Lees. Keeping a watching brief was Traction Inspector Jimmy McClelland. The immediate getaway wasn't particularly fast but the pick up down to Ormside Viaduct was good and as we passed Milepost 275 we were bang on 60mph. It soon became apparent that a special effort was being made and we entered Helm Tunnel at 55mph. The minimum on the first stretch of 1-in-100 was 53½mph

and a sparkling recovery on the easing that followed saw us cross Smardale Viaduct at 66mph. The next stretch of 1-in-100 to Kirkby Stephen could only pull us back to 56½mph and 46229 thundered into the darkness of Birkett Tunnel at 52½. I fancy that she slipped briefly as she went into the tunnel and, for the only time on the climb, speed dropped below 50mph as she passed Milepost 264. But the easing to Mallerstang saw speed rise to the mid 50's and now we were on the last stretch of 1-in-100 and with the record within our grasp. What a sight she must have made as the Duchess stormed on up to Ais Gill, speed decaying only very slowly and we stormed past Milepost 260 at 52mph. The level quarter mile that followed saw speed increase to 54mph as we flew past the usual mass of photographers and then there was a chance to quickly check the times to see what we had achieved. And the answer was a staggering new record, 16 minutes 14 seconds, an average of 56.4mph and an improvement of three-quarters of a minute on *Duke of Gloucester*'s time. This quantum leap had called for an average edhp of around 2,180 for 16 minutes and a maximum of close to 2,520 on the final three miles. Coming after 13 minutes of outstanding effort this was truly remarkable. At Garsdale everyone wanted to know if we had broken the record. Jimmy McClelland was smiling broadly and proudly displaying his stop watch which accurately showed the time up from Ormside. I managed to get a word with him and he told me that

Coronation pacifics were affectionelly known as 'Big Lizzies' by the former Upperby and Kingmoor crews, and 46229 was a firm favourite with them; especially when they were chasing a record time with a heavy train. With Willie Alexander on the regulator, *Duchess of Hamilton* leaves Appleby on the 7th January 1984 before setting a new record that was to last for the next 7 years. Photo: Peter Fitton

This was the final steam duty for former Upperby driver Ken Stubbs before his retirement and he certainly intended to go out in a blaze of glory with *Duke of Gloucester* on the 5th February 1994. Running on a poor rail for the first few miles, Ken, assisted by fireman Gordon Hodgson, produced a blistering performance with 71000 on the climb through Mallerstang and on towards the summit - missing the record by a mere six seconds. Tongue-in-cheek, they will remind you that they remained within the line speed limit of 60mph throughout the climb.

most of the climb had been done on full regulator and 55% cut-off. Both injectors had been on the whole time and the pressure gauge had been rock steady on 250p.s.i. An amazing effort and the Duchess had made her point. How would the others respond?

The 'Duke' responds

The Duke's response came on 11th December when, driven by Jackie Eden she posted her best time yet at 16 minutes 41 seconds, impressive but still some way behind 46229. At Milepost 268 she had been a few seconds ahead of the Duchess's time but the effort had fallen away somewhat on to Milepost 262 before recovering to match the Duchess on the final 2 miles of climbing. But the Duke still hadn't shown her best.

For some reason I had decided to video 71000's southbound run on 5th February 1994. Had I known that this was the final steam run of Carlisle driver Kenny Stubbs my decision would have been different. I had already got a shot of the train as it passed Howe & Company Sidings and then, in typically soaking S & C weather, went up to the south end of Birkett Tunnel and trekked

out onto the rain swept moors. Covered in mud and thoroughly fed up I waited for the Duke and watched as she burst out of the tunnel as if the very devil was after her. It was obvious that she was going well and the increase in the rapidity of her exhaust note as she accelerated away towards Mallerstang made me begin to think that I was probably missing something special. It was with mixed feelings that I learned later that 71000 and Kenny had missed out by just 6 seconds by virtue of an easier first few miles of the climb. As the Duke had passed Milepost 270 she had been 21 seconds behind record pace, but had then beaten the Duchess's time by 15 seconds over the final 10¼ miles. But 46229's record had survived and would continue to do so.

Other runs

While the majority of runs over the S & C met the requirements for 'Blue Riband' consideration, there

The Blue Riband – Mileposts 275 to 259¾ - The Top Six						
Date	Locomotive	Load Vehs/tare/gross	Driver	Fireman	Time mins.secs	Average mph
14.08.93	46229	12/438/460	Grierson	Kane/Lees	16.14	56.4
05.02.94	71000	12/442/465	Stubbs	Hodgson	16.20	56.0
11.12.93	71000	12/443/472	Eden	Howson	16.41	54.9
20.07.91	71000	12/443/465	Alexander	Kane	17.00	53.8
24.04.93	46229	12/439/455	Eden	Finlinson	17.23	52.6
21.03.92	60532	12/437/473	Alexander	Kane/Hodgson	17.33	52.1

were some that didn't but that were noteworthy in their own way. The fastest single headed climb in preservation was achieved by John Cameron's A4 60009 on 16th November 1991 with a load of only 8 vehicles of 325 tons gross. A familiar name, Willie Alexander was at the controls and took the A4 over the 'Blue Riband' section in just 15 minutes 42 seconds, passing Milepost 260 at 59mph. And on 31st July 1993 another A4, *Sir Nigel Gresley*, matched 46229's record time of 16 minutes 14 seconds but with 10 coaches of 385 tons gross. The driver on this occasion was Jackie Eden and the minimum at the summit was 53mph.

The need for sustained power dictated that single chim-

neyed locomotives didn't figure at the very top of the record lists but this didn't stop them trying. Indeed, a particular favourite of mine, *Princess Margaret Rose*, became one of the most consistent performers on the 'Drag'. Kenny Stubbs was a great believer in 46203 and, on one famous occasion, even though booked non-stop through Appleby, stopped momentarily lest he break the record and be accused of having a rolling start. That was on 'The Westmorelander' tour on 4th October 1991. Kenny's time that day was 18 minutes 51 seconds. The 'Princess' went on to set the single chimneyed record some 3 years later when, on 28th May 1994, driven by Paul Kane and fired by Gordon Hodgson and a certain Howard Routledge, she posted a time of 18 minutes 41 seconds

Mileposts 275 to 259¾ - Other notable runs						
Date	Locomotive	Load Vehs/tare/gross	Driver	Time mins.secs	Average mph	Comments
16.11.91	60009	8/311/325	Alexander	15.42	58.3	Fastest known single headed preservation ascent.
31.07.93	4498	10/364/385	Eden	16.14	56.4	Equals 'Blue Riband' record but with lighter load.
21.10.06	71000	13/473/505	Kirk	17.51	51.3	Record for 13 coach load.
28.05.94	46203	12/439/470	Kane	18.41	49.0	'Blue Riband' record for single chimneyed locomotive.
30.05.83	46229	14/533/560	Tickner	19.25	47.1	Record for 14 coach load.

Class A2 No. 60532 *Blue Peter* was certainly in contention for taking the 'Blue Riband' until it was discovered that the injectors couldn't keep up with the demands of the boiler. On the attempt dated 21st March 1992, the locomotive was certainly on target as she passed Smardale, but by Kirkby Stephen the water level in the boiler began to drop so much that Driver Willie Alexander had no other option but to ease the position of the reverser, which obviously ended any further interest in the event. This problem had become evident in tests on the 'Aberdonian' in 1951, but Doncaster never considered increasing the injector cone diameters fitted to the class.

The fastest climb in preservation years belongs to A4 No. 60009 *Union of South Africa*, but because the load was only eight coaches, the run was well outside the parameters of the Blue Riband event. On 16th November 1991, 60009 negotiates Petteril Bridge Junction with her eight coach train with Driver Willie Alexander once again at the controls.

The end of the 'Blue Riband'

The challenge for the 'Riband' ended in the mid 90's, some in 'authority' claiming to have ended it officially in late 1993, citing speeding as the reason. This betrays a lack of knowledge for, on the vast majority of runs there was no infringement of the 60mph limit. And on those that did, it was usually no more than 62 or 63mph at Ormside Viaduct. No, I fancy that these people attached powers to themselves that they didn't have and the fact that two of the top 6 come after the date of their pronouncement confirms this. There were other reasons for the demise of the competition. 1994 saw the withdrawal of 60532 after the incident at Durham and within another 2 years, the Duke and Duchess had also left the scene. There was simply no locomotive left that could challenge for the title. No competitors, no contest. And then the S & C itself began to show the inevitable signs of years of neglect with the appearance of numerous long term temporary speed restrictions from which it is only now recovering. So the death of the 'Blue Riband' contest was a natural event rather than man-made.

A 'Blue Riband' revival?

And what of the future, will we see the contest revived? The main line is now graced by a different Duchess, 46233 and the Duke is back once again. But the Settle & Carlisle Line is still subject to many restrictions which is likely to deny them a crack at the title. There is little room for improvement on *Duchess of Hamilton's* time and conditions would have to be perfect for any locomotive to do so. But we should never say never and, on 21st October 2006, 71000 set a new mark for a 13 coach train, beating *Duchess of Hamilton's* 22 year old record by some 5 seconds. So far that appears to have been a one-off and my feeling is that the 14th August 1993 probably marked the pinnacle of steam's achievement on the 'Long Drag'.

The 'Blue Riband' contest was born out of pride. The pride that footplatemen have in their ability. The pride that owning groups have in their locomotives and the pleasure in demonstrating that that pride is well founded. It's a quality that is endemic in steam and long may it remain so.

It will be noted that all of the major players in this event are of the double-chimney variety, but here we see *Princess Margaret Rose* storming through Kirkby Stephen on the 28th May 1994 whilst making her best-ever time on the climb. Just prior to departure from Appleby, Gordon Hodgson asked if I would fire the locomotive up the bank; he obviously had an inkling of what Driver Paul Kane was to deliver. It soon became obvious that Paul was in a hurry and I can honestly say that it was the first and only time that I had the inclination to wander across to the driver's side of the cab in order to check the position of the reverser, and guess what - it was exactly where I thought it was! Photo: Peter Fitton

Setting a new record for a 13 coach train on 21st October 2006, 71000 *Duke of Gloucester* clears Ais Gill Viaduct on the final approach to the summit. With the sanders being employed on what appears to be a dry rail, Driver Peter Kirk was obviously not taking any chances.

Chapter Seven – Steam's Future on the S&C

The preserved steam locomotive has been a permanent feature of the Settle & Carlisle Railway for over thirty glorious years, but what of the future. Can enthusiasts reasonably expect that steam locomotives will still be climbing the grades towards Ais Gill summit in say ten or twenty year's time? As long as steam doesn't seriously blot its copy book, and there is still a healthy demand for tickets, it would seem that only operational matters will stand in the way of its continued presence on the line.

To some, it would appear incredulous, that a good number of the locomotives that have been regular performers on the S&C throughout the past 30 years are now over 70, and in some cases, over 80 years old, and it would seem appropriate to question as to how long they can go on. The steam engineer would, no doubt, point out that the steam locomotive has to pass the same mechanical tests, and more, as the modern railway vehicle. To retain its 'main-line ticket', a steam locomotive is usually due to be stripped down and rebuilt every seven years, a requisite more for the boiler than it's mechanical condition. In addition to this, there are annual boiler and mechanical examinations, and like all railway vehicles, they have to pass the 'fitness to run' exam prior to each appearance on the main line. The modern railway has also thrown up additional requirements, and steam has adapted to each and every one of them, be it replacing the Automatic Warning System (AWS) with the Train Protection Warning System (TPWS), or the fitting of On Train Monitor Recorders (OTMR), or to cater for the near demise of the vacuum brake with the costly installation of air braking equipment.

One method to ensure that locomotives don't expire through old-age has recently been displayed at Darlington with the building of a brand new steam locomotive; Class A1 No. 60163 *Tornado*, which entered traffic as the year 2008 came to a close. Perhaps this is the way forward to guarantee steam's long term future on the main line.

But in addition to the locomotives, we should also reflect on the situation concerning members of support crews, the majority of which, no doubt, will be coming up to retirement age. Will those in that particular age group look forward to another major overhaul lasting a number of years, (and the huge expense of it), to be followed by another seven year period of main line running. Although younger members have appeared on the scene, the majority of crew members do tend to have acquired their interest prior to the demise of steam from British Railways (1968), and added to this concern of course, is the continued availability of main line steam crews.

Although we tend to focus on the locomotives, it will undoubtedly be these human issues that will eventually decide steam's long term future.

But what of the S&C itself. The line is certainly in a more healthy state than ever before with an increase in traffic year on year. Major engineering work has recently taken place which has more or less included the complete relaying of the southbound (up) line to cater for heavily laden coal trains. These are projected to increase in volume as additional trains are transferred from the West Coast Main Line. To make provision for this increase in traffic, Network Rail have recently installed a number of Intermediate Block signals on the route which have shortened several signal block sections, especially the two extraordinarily long ones that existed, from Settle Junction to Blea Moor, and between Low House Crossing and Culgaith.

As use of the line increases further, the knock-on effect for steam-hauled charter trains will obviously be the sourcing of suitable paths, which all seems a long way from the situation that we had during the 1980s when the route hosted only four trains per day. But of course those were the days when senior management within BR was intent on closing the line.

To appreciate what the future holds, we should look back to 1T57, or to be more precise, the 40th anniversary of that 'final' steam-hauled train. On the 10th August 2008, Britannia No. 70013 *Oliver Cromwell* returned to main line action after a forty year absence with a re-run of the infamous 1T57. Its appearance on the line was to herald an amazing eight day period which witnessed a total of three steam locomotives (45231, 46115 and 70013) making their preserved debuts on the route, whilst Jubilee 5690 *Leander* returned after an absence of twenty-three years. As we entered the 4th decade of steam workings on the line, the majority of charter trains were hauled by this quartet in addition to three trains that featured new-build 60163 *Tornado*. With these five locomotives joining an already strong pool of steam traction familiar with the S&C, coupled with the enterprising tour proposals recently witnessed on the line, steam's future on the Settle to Carlisle Railway looks very positive indeed.

After having been involved with BR's final steam hauled train in August 1968, Britannia 70013 *Oliver Cromwell* returned to the main line after a forty year absence in time to once again display the 1T57 train reporting number on the S&C. The 2008 commemorative train is pictured on the approach to Langwathby on the 10th August as 70013 heads north with the Manchester Victoria-Carlisle leg - just as it did in 1968.

In order to mirror the 1968 event, the southbound working featured a double-headed Black Five combination, and after the 2008 train had arrived at Carlisle, 70013 was quickly turned before returning to the station to pose alongside 45407 and 45231. The 1T57 train reporting number attached to 45407 was a 1968 original, having been displayed on 44871 on that historic day. Photo: Peter Fitton

Another view of 1T57 as 45407 and 45231 arrive at the Appleby water stop on the 10th August 2008. In addition to 70013, 45231 was also making its preservation debut on the S&C that day.

Another locomotive to return to the main line during 2008 was Carnforth based Royal Scot class No. 46115 *Scots Guardsman*. This locomotive was no stranger to the S&C as it had been allocated to Carlisle Kingmoor shed until its withdrawal from service at the end of 1965, an event which made the class extinct on BR metals. Although the locomotive had returned to main line running during 1978, this was restricted to only two trains before it became nothing more than a static exhibit at a number of railway centres that included Dinting, Tyseley and Crewe. It was not until thirty years later that a Royal Scot was heard once again in the Cumbrian fells where 46115 is pictured on the 7th February 2009 climbing hard at Birkett Common on a snow-covered S&C.

In a scene that could be placed in the latter part of the 1950s, 46115 *Scots Guardsman* passes Breaks Hall with a southbound Cumbrian Mountain Express on the 2nd August 2009. The southern approach to Helm Tunnel can be seen in the background.

Later that same month, 70013 *Oliver Cromwell* crosses Bongate Bridge at Appleby with the return working of a CME from Carlisle to York. Once again, there is a distinct British Railways feel surrounding this view as a BR liveried engine, a Waverley headboard, and maroon stock, all combine to make an excellent attempt to turn the clock back by some fifty years.

Forty-two years after the last example of the LNER A1 Class was dispatched to the scrap-yard, new-build No. 60163 *Tornado* emerged from its Darlington workshop to herald a new era in the manufacturing of British built standard gauge steam locomotives. Understandably, 60163's inaugural runs were concentrated on the East Coast Main Line, but in October 2009 the locomotive made three appearances on the S&C to become, what I believe, is the 48th steam locomotive to feature on the line since *Green Arrow's* ground-breaking run in 1978. *Tornado* is featured making a cautious climb away from Carlisle on a rain affected S&C on Sunday 4th October 2009 whilst returning the Waverley to York.

Coming to the end of our journey, I feel it prudent that I finish the book with a look at the locomotive that started my association working with steam on the Settle to Carlisle Railway, Stanier class 5X No. 5690 *Leander*.

On the 20th April 1985, 5690 hauled a charter between Kilmarnock and Hellifield. By this time the locomotive had been purchased by the Severn Valley Railway and it was thought by many that this was to be the last run for 5690 on the S&C. This 'final' run was certainly not to be forgotten as upon arrival at Appleby (pictured top); *Leander* – already running late - had to clear the main line by propelling its train onto one of the two roads beside the signal box. The reason for this manoeuvre was to allow the passage of a diesel locomotive that had been summoned from Carlisle to assist a failed service train at Crosby Garrett. After the passage of the light engine, matters got rather busy at Appleby when a diesel-hauled charter came to a stand at signals on the up line on the opposite side of the box to us. Once the up line was clear there would be no doubt as to who would be the first to be released from Appleby, and sure enough it was the diesel-hauled train.

After a delay of two hours, *Leander* was eventually given the road prior to Driver David Gardner giving a performance on the climb to the summit, few who witnessed, will ever forget; the cinders were certainly cold when they were landing on the coach roofs.

Fast-forward twenty-three years, and 5690 - now under new ownership, made a welcome return to the line in 2008 and is pictured (bottom) on Sunday 9th August 2009 passing the preserved signal box at Armathwaite station, the exact location where my association with steam had begun some 27 years previously, when I was accosted to purchase those Christmas draw tickets.

Appendix

Steam Locomotives featured on the S&C since 1978

LMS

41000 (1000)
42968 (2968)
44767 (4767)
44871
44932
45231
45305 (5305)
45407 (5407)
45593 (5593) Kolhapur
45596 Bahamas
45690 (5690) Leander
46115 Scots Guardsman
46201 (6201) Princess Elizabeth
46203 Princess Margaret Rose
46229 Duchess of Hamilton
46233 (6233) Duchess of Sutherland
46441
48151
48773

LNER

60007 (4498) Sir Nigel Gresley
60009 Union of South Africa
60022 (4468) Mallard
60103 (4472) Flying Scotsman
60163 Tornado
60532 Blue Peter
60800 (4771) Green Arrow
61264 (1264)
61994 (3442) The Great Marquess
62005 (2005)
65243 (673) Maude

GWR

5029 Nunney Castle
5972 Olton Hall
6024 King Edward I

SR

30777 (777) Sir Lamiel
30828 (828)
30850 (850) Lord Nelson
34027 Taw Valley
34067 Tangmere
34092 City of Wells
35005 Canadian Pacific
35028 Clan Line

BR Standard

70000 Britannia
70013 Oliver Cromwell
71000 Duke of Gloucester
75014
76079
80080
92220 Evening Star